WOMEN AND REAL ESTATE

How Women Can Outsmart the Competition and
Win in the Real Estate Market

TYLER GIBSON

Copyright

No part of this book may be reproduced in any written, electronic, recording, or photocopying without the publisher's or author's written permission.

The exception would be in the case of brief quotations embodied in the critical articles or reviews and pages where the publisher or author specifically grants permission.

Although every precaution has been taken to verify the accuracy of the information contained herein, the author and publisher assume no responsibility for any errors or omissions. No liability is assumed for damages that may result from the use of the information contained within.

Contents

Chapter 1: Women in Real Estate: A Historical Perspective

1.1. The evolution of women in real estate

Women have been involved in the real estate industry since its inception in the late 18th century. However, their roles were initially limited to administrative and supportive positions. It wasn't until the early 20th century that women began to break into the male-dominated field of real estate sales and brokerage.

One of the pioneers of the women's movement in real estate was Elizabeth Arden, who founded the Elizabeth Arden Realty Company in 1920. Arden was a successful businesswoman and entrepreneur, and she used her platform to promote gender equality in the workplace. She was also one of the first real estate brokers to target female clients.

Another trailblazer of the women's movement in real estate was Daisy Bates, who became the first African-American woman to earn a real estate license in Arkansas in 1948. Bates was a civil rights activist who used her real estate business to help Black families find homes in white neighborhoods. She was also a vocal advocate for fair housing legislation.

In the 1950s and 1960s, the women's movement in real estate began to gain momentum. More and more women were entering the field, and they were starting to achieve success in leadership roles. In 1973, the National Association of Realtors (NAR) began admitting female sales associates, and by 1978, women made up the majority of NAR members.

In recent decades, women have continued to make progress in the real estate industry. Today, women represent over 65% of all Realtors in the United States. They are also well-represented in leadership positions, with women holding over 40% of the top executive positions at real estate companies.

The evolution of women in real estate has been a remarkable one. From humble beginnings in the late 19th century, women have risen to become the driving force of the industry today. Their success is a testament to their hard work, determination, and perseverance.

Key milestones in the evolution of women in real estate:

- 1893: Elizabeth Arden becomes the first woman to earn a real estate license in New York City.
- 1920: Elizabeth Arden founded the Elizabeth Arden Realty Company.
- 1948: Daisy Bates becomes the first African American woman to earn a real estate license in Arkansas.
- 1960s: Women begin to enter the real estate industry in large numbers and achieve success in leadership roles.
- 1973: The National Association of Realtors (NAR) begins admitting female sales associates.
- 1978: Women become the majority of NAR members.
- 1992: NAR elects its first female president.
- Today: Women represent over 65% of all Realtors in the United States and hold over 40% of the top executive positions at real estate companies.

The evolution of women in real estate has been a remarkable one, and it continues today. Women are making significant contributions to the industry in all areas, from sales and brokerage to development and financing. As the industry continues to evolve, women will be at the forefront of change.

1.2. The challenges and opportunities facing women in real estate today

Challenges Facing Women in Real Estate Today

Women have made significant progress in the real estate industry in recent decades. However, they still face a number of challenges, including:

1. Gender discrimination:

Gender discrimination is one of the biggest challenges facing women in real estate today. It can manifest itself in a variety of ways, including:

a. Pay discrimination: Women in real estate are often paid less than men for doing the same work. A 2022 study by the National Association of Realtors found that the median income for female real estate agents was $89,900, compared to $120,500 for male real estate agents.

b. Overlooking for promotions and leadership positions: Women are often overlooked for promotions and leadership positions in the real estate industry. A 2021 study by McKinsey & Company found that women make up only 22% of senior leadership positions in the real estate industry.

c. Harassment and sexism: Women in real estate are often subjected to harassment and sexism, both from clients and from other professionals in the industry. A 2022 survey by the National Association of Realtors found that 42% of female real estate agents had experienced sexual harassment at some point in their careers.

Gender discrimination can have a significant impact on women's careers in real estate. It can lead to lower earnings, fewer opportunities for advancement, and a hostile work environment.

2. Work-life balance:

Work-life balance is a challenge for many women in real estate, due to the demanding nature of the industry. Real estate agents often work long hours, including evenings and weekends, to meet the needs of their clients. They may also have to travel frequently to show properties and meet with clients. This can make it difficult for women in real estate to maintain a healthy work-life balance, especially if they have families.

Several factors contribute to the work-life balance challenges faced by women in real estate. One factor is the gendered expectations placed on women in the workplace. Women are often expected to be primary caregivers for their children and families, even if they are also working full-time jobs. This can make it difficult for women in real estate to prioritize their work without feeling guilty about neglecting their families.

Another factor that contributes to the work-life balance challenges faced by women in real estate is the lack of flexible work arrangements in the industry. Many real estate firms do not offer flexible work arrangements, such as telecommuting or part-time work. This can make it difficult for women in real estate to balance their work and family responsibilities.

Finally, the competitive nature of the real estate industry can also contribute to work-life balance challenges for women. Real estate agents often feel pressure to work long hours and be available to clients at all times in order to be successful. This can make it difficult for women in real estate to maintain a healthy work-life balance.

3. Safety concerns:

Women in real estate are often required to work alone and meet with strangers in unfamiliar locations. This can make them particularly vulnerable to safety risks. According to a 2022 survey by the National Association of Realtors, 45% of female real estate agents have experienced some form of sexual harassment or assault while on the job.

Here are some of the specific safety concerns that women in real estate face:

a. Meeting with strangers in unfamiliar locations: Women in real estate often need to meet with clients to show them properties or discuss their real estate needs. This can involve meeting with strangers in unfamiliar locations, such as vacant homes or deserted parking lots.

b. Working late at night: Women in real estate may need to work late at night to accommodate their clients' schedules. This can be especially dangerous if they are working in an unfamiliar area or traveling alone.

c. Carrying cash and valuables: Women in real estate often carry cash and valuables, such as jewelry and expensive electronic devices. This can make them a target for criminals.

d. Being perceived as vulnerable: Women in real estate may be perceived as being more vulnerable than men, which can make them more likely to be targeted by criminals.

Opportunities for Women in Real Estate Today

1. Growing demand for women real estate agents:

The growing demand for women real estate agents is one of the most exciting opportunities for women in the real estate industry today. According to a recent study by the National Association of Realtors (NAR), women make up 64% of all real estate agents in the United States. This number has been steadily increasing in recent years, and it is expected to continue to grow in the future.

There are a number of factors contributing to the growing demand for women real estate agents. One factor is that more and more women are buying and selling homes. In fact, women are now the primary homebuyers in the United States. When women are buying or selling a home, they are often looking for a real estate agent who they can trust and who understands their needs. Many women feel more comfortable working with a woman real estate agent, as they feel like they can relate to them better and that they will be more understanding of their unique needs.

Another factor contributing to the growing demand for women real estate agents is that women are increasingly taking on leadership roles in the real estate industry. In the past, the real estate industry was largely dominated by men. However, this is changing rapidly. Today, there are more women leaders in the real estate industry than ever before. This is opening up new opportunities for women to advance their careers and to become successful real estate agents.

Finally, technology is making it easier for women to start and manage their own real estate businesses. In the past, starting a real estate business was a daunting task. However, today there are a number of online tools and resources that can help women get started quickly and easily. This is making it possible for more women to pursue a career in real estate and to achieve their financial goals.

The growing demand for women real estate agents is a great opportunity for women who are interested in a career in the real estate industry. Women who are resourceful, resilient, and determined can achieve great success in this field.

2. Increasing opportunities for women leaders:

One of the most significant opportunities for women in real estate today is the increasing opportunities for women leaders. There are a number of factors that are contributing to this trend, including:

a. Changing demographics: The real estate industry is becoming more diverse, with more women and minorities entering the field. This is creating a demand for more diverse leadership.

b. Focus on diversity and inclusion: Many companies are now making a concerted effort to promote diversity and inclusion in the workplace. This is leading to more opportunities for women to advance into leadership positions.

c. Mentorship and sponsorship programs: There are a growing number of mentorship and sponsorship programs designed to help women advance into leadership positions in real estate. These programs can provide women with the support and guidance they need to succeed.

d. Women's leadership organizations: There are a number of women's leadership organizations in the real estate industry, such as CREW Network and Women's Council of REALTORS®. These organizations can provide women with opportunities to network with other women leaders, learn from experienced mentors, and develop their leadership skills.

As a result of these trends, there are more women in leadership positions in real estate than ever before. For example, according to the National Association of Realtors®, women account for 51% of all real estate agents in the United States. Additionally, women now hold 25% of all leadership positions in the National Association of Realtors.

This is good news for women in real estate, as it means that there are more opportunities for them to advance into leadership positions and have a greater impact on the industry. It is also good news for the real estate industry as a whole, as having more women in leadership positions can lead to more diverse and inclusive workplaces, better decision-making, and improved performance.

Here are some specific examples of the increasing opportunities for women leaders in real estate today:

- More women are being appointed to CEO and board positions at real estate companies. For example, in 2022, CBRE appointed its first female CEO, Jane Fraser. Additionally, the number of women on the boards of real estate companies has increased significantly in recent years.
- More women are starting their real estate businesses. For example, in 2021, women-owned real estate businesses generated $1.4 trillion in revenue in the United States. This is a significant increase from 2016 when women-owned real estate businesses generated $987 billion in revenue.
- More women are serving in leadership positions in real estate industry organizations. For example, the National Association of Realtors® has several women serving in

leadership positions, including the President, CEO, and Treasurer.

These are just a few examples of the increasing opportunities for women leaders in real estate today. As the industry continues to evolve and become more diverse, we can expect to see even more women in leadership positions in the years to come.

3. Technology:

Technology is one of the biggest opportunities for women in real estate today. It is making it easier for women to start and manage their nesses, connect with clients and other professionals, and stay up-to-date on the latest trends and information.

Here are some of the specific ways that technology is helping women succeed in real estate:

a. Social media: Social media platforms like LinkedIn, Twitter, and Facebook can be used to market and promote a real estate business, connect with potential clients and other professionals, and build relationships. Women can use social media to share their expertise, provide valuable content, and engage with their followers.

b. Online tools: There are a number of online tools that can help women manage their real estate businesses more efficiently and effectively. For example, customer relationship management (CRM) software can help women track leads, manage their pipeline, and communicate with clients.

c. Virtual tours: Virtual tours allow women to showcase properties to potential clients without having to be there in person. This can be especially helpful for women who are working with clients who live far away or who are unable to visit properties in person.

d. E-signatures: E-signatures allow women to sign and send documents electronically, which can save time and hassle.

f. Online education: Several online courses and programs can help women learn about real estate and develop their skills. This can be a great way for women to get started in the industry or to advance their careers.

Overall, technology is giving women in real estate more opportunities than ever before. By leveraging technology, women can start and manage their own businesses, connect with clients and other professionals, and stay up-to-date on the latest trends and information.

Here are some specific examples of how women in real estate are using technology to succeed:

- One real estate agent uses social media to share her expertise on the local market and to connect with potential clients. She regularly posts blog articles, videos, and infographics about topics such as home buying, selling, and investing. She also uses social media to engage with her followers and answer their questions.
- Another real estate agent uses CRM software to track her leads and manage her pipeline. She uses the software to automate tasks such as sending follow-up emails and scheduling appointments. This frees up her time so that she can focus on building relationships with clients and closing deals.
- Another real estate agent uses virtual tours to showcase properties to potential clients who live far away or who

are unable to visit properties in person. She creates high-quality virtual tours that allow clients to walk through a property at their own pace and get a feel for the layout and features.

- Another real estate agent uses e-signatures to send and sign documents electronically. This saves her time and hassle, and it also makes it easier for her to close deals with clients who live far away.
- Another real estate agent took an online course to learn about real estate investing. After completing the course, she started investing in rental properties. She now has a portfolio of rental properties that provide her with a steady income.

These are just a few examples of how women in real estate are using technology to succeed. Technology is giving women more opportunities than ever before to start and manage their usinesses, connect with clients and other professionals, and stay up-to-date on the latest trends and information.

4. Supportive organizations:

Supportive organizations for women in real estate are a valuable resource for women who are looking to build their careers in the industry. These organizations can provide women with networking opportunities, professional development, and support.

One of the most important benefits of supportive organizations is that they can help women network with other women in the industry. Networking is essential for building relationships, generating leads, and finding mentors and sponsors. Supportive organizations often host networking events, such as luncheons, dinners, and conferences. These events provide women with the opportunity to meet other women in real estate, learn from their experiences, and share their own stories.

Another important benefit of supportive organizations is that they can provide women with professional development opportunities. Many supportive organizations offer workshops, seminars, and other educational programs on topics such as real estate marketing, negotiation, and investing. These programs can help women to develop the skills and knowledge they need to succeed in the real estate industry.

In addition to networking and professional development opportunities, supportive organizations can also provide women with support. Women in real estate often face unique challenges, such as gender discrimination, work-life balance issues, and safety concerns. Supportive organizations can provide women with a safe space to share their experiences, get advice and support from other women, and find resources to help them overcome these challenges.

Some of the most well-known supportive organizations for women in real estate include:

- CREW Network
- Women's Council of REALTORS®
- National Association of Women in Real Estate Businesses (NAWRB)
- National Women's Homeownership Coalition (NWHC)
- Urban Land Institute (ULI) Women's Leadership Initiative
- Women's Real Estate Investors Association (WREIA)

These organizations offer a variety of resources and support to women in real estate, including networking opportunities, professional development programs, and advocacy. Women who are interested in a career in real estate should consider joining one or more of these organizations to take advantage of the many benefits they offer.

Here are some specific examples of how supportive organizations can help women in real estate:

- A woman who is new to the real estate industry may join a supportive organization to meet other women in the industry and learn about different career paths.
- A woman who is struggling to balance her work with her family life may join a supportive organization to get advice and support from other women who are facing similar challenges.
- A woman who is interested in investing in real estate may join a supportive organization to learn about different types of real estate investments and how to get started.
- A woman who is facing gender discrimination at work may join a supportive organization to get advice on how to handle the situation and to find support from other women who have faced similar experiences.

Overall, supportive organizations are a valuable resource for women in real estate. They can provide women with networking opportunities, professional development, and support, which can help them overcome the challenges they face and achieve their goals in the industry.

1.3. How women are outsmarting the competition and winning in the real estate market

Here are some of the ways that women are outsmarting the competition and winning in the real estate market:

1. Networking: Networking is one of the most important ways that women are outsmarting the competition and winning in the real estate market. Networking allows women to build relationships with other women in the industry, learn from each other, share resources, and generate referrals.

There are several ways that women can network in the real estate industry. Some of the most effective ways include:

a. Joining professional organizations: There are a number of professional organizations for women in real estate, such as CREW Network and Women's Council of REALTORS®. These organizations offer a variety of networking opportunities, such as events, online forums, and mentoring programs.

b. Attending industry events: Industry events are a great way to meet other women in real estate and to learn about the latest trends and developments in the market. Some popular industry events include the National Association of Realtors® Conference and Expo and the Inman Connect Conference.

c. Connecting with other women on social media: social media is a powerful tool for networking with other women in real estate. Women can use social media to connect with other women in their local area, to join professional groups, and to share their expertise and insights.

Here are some specific examples of how networking has helped women to succeed in the real estate market:

- One-woman real estate agent was able to close a $1 million deal after meeting a potential buyer at a networking event. The buyer was looking for a real estate agent who specialized in working with investors, and the woman real estate agent had just started specializing in this area.

- Another woman real estate agent was able to land a job at a top brokerage after being referred by a contact she met at a professional organization event. The contact had been impressed with the woman real estate agent's knowledge and expertise, and she recommended her to the hiring manager at the brokerage.
- A group of women real estate agents in a small town formed a networking group to support each other and to share resources. The group meets regularly to discuss their businesses, to learn about new market trends, and to refer clients to each other.

Overall, networking is an essential part of success for women in the real estate industry. By networking with other women in the industry, women can learn from each other, share resources, and generate referrals.

2. Mentorship: Mentorship is one of the most important ways that women are outsmarting the competition and winning in the real estate market. A mentor is a trusted advisor who can provide guidance, support, and advice to a mentee. A mentor can help a mentee to develop their skills and knowledge, to navigate the industry, and to achieve their career goals.

Mentorship is especially important for women in the real estate industry, which is still dominated by men. A mentor can help a woman to overcome the challenges that she may face, such as gender discrimination, lack of access to capital, and work-life balance issues. A mentor can also help a woman to develop her confidence and to build her network.

Here are some of the specific ways that mentorship can help women to succeed in the real estate market:

- Help women to develop their skills and knowledge. A mentor can provide a woman with training and coaching on a variety of topics, such as real estate law, marketing, and negotiation. A mentor can also help a woman to develop her soft skills, such as communication, leadership, and teamwork.
- Help women to navigate the industry. A mentor can help a woman to understand the different career paths in real estate and to identify the best path for her. A mentor can also help a woman to network with other people in the industry and to find job opportunities.
- Help women to achieve their career goals. A mentor can help a woman to set and achieve her career goals. A mentor can also provide a woman with support and encouragement along the way.

3. Technology: Technology is rapidly changing the real estate industry, and women are at the forefront of this change. Women are using technology to outsmart the competition and win in the real estate market in several ways, including:

a. Marketing their businesses: Women are using social media to market their businesses more effectively than men. A study by the National Association of Realtors found that women real estate agents are more likely to use social media for marketing than men, and they are also more likely to use it effectively. The study found that women real estate agents who use social media for marketing generate more leads and sales than those who do not.

Some of the specific ways that women are using social media to market their businesses include:

- Creating and sharing high-quality content, such as blog posts, infographics, and videos, that is relevant to their target audience
- Running targeted social media ads
- Engaging with their followers on social media by responding to comments and questions
- Using social media to connect with other real estate professionals and potential clients

b. Managing their businesses: Women are also using technology to manage their businesses more efficiently than men. A study by the National Association of Female Executives found that women business owners are more likely to use online tools to manage their businesses than men. The study found that women business owners who use online tools are more likely to be successful.

Some of the specific online tools that women are using to manage their businesses include:

- Customer relationship management (CRM) software to track and manage their leads and clients
- Project management software to track and manage their projects
- Accounting software to track and manage their finances
- Marketing automation software to automate their marketing tasks

c. Providing better customer service: Women are also using technology to provide better customer service to their clients. For example, they are using video conferencing to give virtual tours of homes, and they are using electronic signatures to make it easier for clients to sign contracts.

d. Staying informed about the market: Women are also using technology to stay informed about the latest trends and developments in the real estate market. For example, they are using real estate market research tools to track property values and market trends. They are also using social media to connect with other real estate professionals and learn from their insights.

Overall, technology is giving women a competitive advantage in the real estate market. By using technology to market their businesses more effectively, manage their businesses more efficiently, provide better customer service, and stay informed about the market, women are able to outsmart the competition and win.

Here are some specific examples of how women are using technology to outsmart the competition and win in the real estate market:

- One-woman real estate agent in New York City is using virtual reality (VR) to give virtual tours of homes to potential buyers. This allows potential buyers to see homes from all over the world without having to travel.
- Another woman real estate agent in Los Angeles is using artificial intelligence (AI) to generate leads. The AI software analyzes data from a variety of sources, such as public records and social media, to identify potential leads.
- A woman real estate broker in Miami is using a blockchain-based platform to make it easier for clients to buy and sell homes. The platform allows clients to track the progress of their purchase or sale in real time and to sign contracts electronically.

These are just a few examples of how women are using technology to outsmart the competition and win in the real estate market. As technology continues to evolve, women will continue to find new and innovative ways to use it to their advantage.

4. Specialization: Specialization is one of the key ways that women are outsmarting the competition and winning in the real estate market. By specializing in a particular area of the market, women are able to develop deep expertise, which makes them more valuable to their clients.

There are many different ways to specialize in the real estate market. Some women specialize in working with a particular type of buyer, such as first-time homebuyers, investors, or luxury home buyers. Others specialize in working with a particular type of seller, such as sellers who are downsizing, relocating, or facing foreclosure. Still others specialize in a particular type of property, such as single-family homes, condos, or commercial properties.

Here are some of the benefits of specializing in the real estate market:

a. Deeper expertise: When women specialize in a particular area of the market, they are able to develop a deep understanding of that market. This includes understanding the specific needs and wants of buyers and sellers in that market, as well as the latest trends and developments.

b. Increased credibility: Women who specialize in a particular area of the market are seen as more credible and knowledgeable by their clients. This is because they have a proven track record of success in that market.

c. Stronger relationships: Women who specialize in a particular area of the market are more likely to develop strong relationships with their clients. This is because they are able to provide their clients with a level of service and expertise that is unmatched by generalists.

d. More referrals: Women who specialize in a particular area of the market are more likely to receive referrals from their clients. This is because their clients are confident that they will provide their friends, family, and colleagues with the same high level of service and expertise.

Here are some examples of how women are using specialization to succeed in the real estate market:

- A woman who specializes in working with first-time homebuyers might offer a free consultation to first-time homebuyers to discuss their needs and budget. She might also host workshops or seminars on home buying for first-time homebuyers.
- A woman who specializes in working with investors might offer a free investment property analysis to investors. She might also host networking events for investors or provide investors with access to exclusive listings.
- A woman who specializes in working with luxury home buyers might offer a free home staging consultation to luxury home sellers. She might also host open houses for luxury homes or provide luxury home buyers with access to exclusive listings.

By specializing in a particular area of the real estate market, women can develop deep expertise, which makes them more valuable to their clients. This can lead to increased sales, more referrals, and a more successful and rewarding career in real estate.

5. Customer service: Customer service is one of the most important ways that women are outsmarting the competition and winning in the real estate market. Women are known for providing excellent customer service, which is essential for building strong relationships with clients and earning their trust.

Here are some of the ways that women are providing excellent customer service in the real estate market:

a. Responsiveness: Women are responsive to their clients' needs. They return phone calls and emails promptly, and they are available to answer their clients' questions and concerns.

b. Knowledge: Women are knowledgeable about the real estate market. They can provide their clients with information about different neighborhoods, schools, and other factors that are important to their clients when buying or selling a home.

c. Commitment: Women are committed to helping their clients achieve their real estate goals. They take the time to understand their client's needs and wants, and they work hard to find the right home or buyer for their clients.

In addition to these general principles of excellent customer service, women are also using some specific strategies to outsmart the competition in the real estate market. For example, some women are using social media to provide their clients with real-time updates on the market and to answer their questions promptly. Other women are using technology to streamline the real estate process and to make it easier for their clients to buy or sell a home.

Here are some specific examples of how women are using customer service to outsmart the competition and win in the real estate market:

- One-woman real estate agent uses social media to provide her clients with real-time updates on the market. She posts about new listings, price changes, and other important news. She also uses social media to answer her clients' questions and to provide them with tips and advice.
- Another woman real estate agent uses technology to streamline the real estate process for her clients. She uses online tools to help her clients find homes, to schedule appointments, and to submit offers. She also uses technology to keep her clients informed of the progress of their transaction.
- A third woman real estate agent is known for her commitment to her clients. She goes above and beyond to help her clients achieve their real estate goals. For example, she has helped her clients to find financing, to negotiate repairs, and to move into their new homes.

Overall, women are using customer service to outsmart the competition and win in the real estate market by being responsive to their clients' needs, being knowledgeable about the market, and being committed to helping their clients achieve their real estate goals.

In addition to the above, here are some other ways that women can use customer service to outsmart the competition in the real estate market:

a. Personalize the experience. Take the time to get to know your clients and their individual needs. This will help you to provide them with the best possible service.

b. Be proactive. Don't wait for your clients to come to you with their questions and concerns. Reach out to them regularly to keep them updated on the progress of their transaction and to offer your assistance.

c. Go the extra mile. Be willing to go above and beyond for your clients. This could involve helping them to find a moving company, to clean out their old home, or to stage their home for sale.

By providing excellent customer service, women can build strong relationships with their clients and earn their trust. This will help them to generate repeat business and referrals, which will lead to long-term success in the real estate market.

Overall, women are outsmarting the competition and winning in the real estate market by networking, finding mentors, using technology to their advantage, specializing in certain areas of the market, and providing excellent customer service.

Chapter 2: The Mindset of a Successful Woman in Real Estate

2.1. Developing a winning mindset

Developing a winning mindset is essential for success in any field, but it is especially important in real estate. The real estate industry is competitive and can be challenging, so it is important to have a positive attitude and to believe in yourself and your abilities.

Here are some tips for developing a winning mindset:

1. Set clear goals: Setting clear goals is one of the most important things that a woman can do to develop a winning mindset in real estate. When you have clear goals, you know what you want to achieve and you have a plan to get there. This can help you to stay focused and motivated, even when things get tough.

Here are some tips for setting clear goals:

1) Make sure your goals are specific, measurable, achievable, relevant, and time-bound. For example, instead of saying "I want to make more money in real estate," set a specific goal like "I want to close 10 deals in the next year."
2) Break down your goals into smaller, more manageable steps. This will make them seem less daunting and help you to track your progress.
3) Write down your goals and put them somewhere where you will see them every day. This will help you to stay focused and motivated.
4) Review your goals regularly and make adjustments as needed. Your goals should be realistic and achievable,

but they should also be challenging enough to push you to grow.

Here is an example of how a woman can set clear goals in real estate:

A woman who is new to the real estate industry may set the following goals:

- Close 10 deals in the next year.
- Increase her commission income by 20%.
- Build a network of 100 potential clients.
- Attend at least one industry event per month.
- Market herself effectively on social media.

These goals are specific, measurable, achievable, relevant, and time-bound. They are also challenging enough to push the woman to grow, but they are also realistic and achievable.

Once the woman has set her goals, she can develop a plan to achieve them. For example, she can create a marketing plan to generate leads, develop a system for tracking her progress, and schedule time each week to network with potential clients.

By setting clear goals and developing a plan to achieve them, the woman can increase her chances of success in the real estate industry.

Here are some additional benefits of setting clear goals:

a. Increased motivation: When you have clear goals, you are more likely to be motivated to achieve them. This is because you know what you are working towards and you have a plan to get there.

b. Improved decision-making: When you have clear goals, you can make better decisions about how to allocate your time and resources. This is because you know what is most important to you and you are focused on achieving your goals.

c. Increased confidence: When you achieve your goals, your confidence increases. This is because you know that you are capable of achieving what you set your mind to.

Overall, setting clear goals is an essential part of developing a winning mindset in real estate. By setting clear goals, women can increase their motivation, improve their decision-making, and increase their confidence.

2. Be positive and believe in yourself: Be positive and believe in yourself is one of the most important things you can do to develop a winning mindset in real estate. When you have a positive attitude and believe in yourself, you are more likely to take on challenges, persevere in the face of setbacks, and achieve your goals.

Here are some tips for being positive and believing in yourself:

1) Focus on your strengths and accomplishments. Make a list of your strengths and accomplishments. Review this list regularly to remind yourself of what you are capable of.

2) Challenge your negative thoughts. When you have a negative thought, ask yourself if it is true. Is there any evidence to support this thought? Or is it just a self-defeating thought that is holding you back?

3) Replace negative thoughts with positive thoughts. When you catch yourself having a negative thought, replace it with a positive thought. For example, instead of thinking "I'm not good enough to be a successful real estate agent," think "I am a smart, capable, and hardworking

individual. I have the skills and knowledge to succeed in real estate."

4) Visualize success. Take some time each day to visualize yourself achieving your goals. See yourself as a successful real estate agent or investor. The more you visualize success, the more likely you are to achieve it.

5) Surround yourself with positive people. The people you spend time with can have a big impact on your mindset. Make sure you are surrounded by positive people who believe in you and your goals.

Here is an example of how a woman can use a positive attitude and belief in herself to succeed in real estate:

- A woman who is new to the real estate industry may be hesitant to approach potential clients because she is afraid of being rejected. However, if she has a positive attitude and believes in herself, she will be more likely to take on this challenge.

- Instead of focusing on the possibility of rejection, the woman can focus on the benefits of networking with potential clients. She can remind herself that she is a knowledgeable and experienced real estate agent who has something to offer potential clients.

- The woman can also visualize herself successfully networking with potential clients. She can see herself making connections with potential clients and building relationships with them.

- By having a positive attitude and believing in herself, the woman is more likely to overcome her fear of rejection and to succeed in networking with potential clients.

- Being positive and believing in yourself is essential for success in any field, but it is especially important in real estate. By developing a positive mindset, you can overcome challenges, achieve your goals, and build a successful career in real estate.

3. Be persistent and never give up.

Persistence is the key to success in any field, but it is especially important in real estate. The real estate industry can be challenging, and there will be times when you want to give up. However, it is important to remember that everyone faces challenges, and the successful people are those who persevere.

Here are some tips for being persistent and never giving up:

Set realistic goals. When you set your goals too high, you are more likely to become discouraged and give up. Set small, achievable goals for yourself, and then celebrate your successes along the way.

Break down large tasks into smaller ones. This will make the tasks seem less daunting and more manageable.

1) Create a plan. Once you have broken down your goals into smaller tasks, create a plan for how you will achieve them.
2) Take action. Don't just sit around and think about what you need to do. Take action and start working towards your goals.
3) Don't be afraid to fail. Everyone fails at some point. It's important to learn from your failures and keep moving forward.
4) Find a support system. Surround yourself with positive people who believe in you and your goals. They can provide you with support and encouragement when you need it most.

Here is an example of how persistence can lead to success in real estate:

A real estate agent is working with a client to sell their home. The market is slow, and the agent has not been able to find any buyers for the home. The agent could easily give up, but she is determined to help her client sell their home.

The agent continues to market the home and to network with potential buyers. She also makes suggestions to the client about how to make the home more appealing to buyers.

After several months, the agent finally finds a buyer for the home. The client is grateful for the agent's persistence and dedication.

This example shows how persistence can lead to success in real estate. The agent never gave up on her client, and she was eventually able to help them sell their home.

Here are some additional tips for being persistent in real estate:

Focus on the long term. Don't get discouraged if you don't see results immediately. It takes time and effort to build a successful real estate career.

Keep learning. The real estate industry is constantly changing, so it is important to keep learning and staying up-to-date on the latest trends and developments.

Don't be afraid to ask for help. If you need help, don't be afraid to ask for it from your mentor, colleagues, or other experienced real estate professionals.

By being persistent and never giving up, you can achieve your goals and succeed in the real estate industry.

4. Surround yourself with positive people: Surrounding yourself with positive people is one of the best ways to develop a winning mindset. Positive people have a contagious attitude and can help you to stay motivated and focused on your goals. They can also offer you support and encouragement when you are facing challenges.

Here are some of the benefits of surrounding yourself with positive people:

a. Positive people can help you to develop a positive attitude. When you spend time with positive people, you are more likely to adopt a positive outlook on life. This can help you to stay motivated and focused on your goals, even when things are tough.

b. Positive people can help you to believe in yourself. Positive people believe in themselves and in their abilities. They can help you to believe in yourself and in your ability to achieve your goals.

c. Positive people can help you to overcome challenges. When you are facing challenges, positive people can offer you support and encouragement. They can help you to see the bright side of things and to stay positive.

d. Positive people can help you to achieve your goals. Positive people are supportive and encouraging. They want to see you succeed. They can help you to stay on track and to achieve your goals.

Here are some tips for surrounding yourself with positive people:

1) Identify the positive people in your life. Think about the people in your life who make you feel good about yourself and who support your goals. Make an effort to spend more time with these people.
2) Meet new people. There are many ways to meet new people, such as joining clubs or groups, attending industry events, or volunteering. When you meet new people, focus on finding those who have a positive attitude and who share your values.
3) Limit your time with negative people. Negative people can drain your energy and bring you down. If there are people in your life who are negative, try to limit your contact with them.

Here is an example of how surrounding yourself with positive people can help you to develop a winning mindset:

A woman is new to the real estate industry and is feeling overwhelmed. She is not sure if she has the skills or experience to be successful. She also has a lot of negative self-talk.

The woman decides to join a networking group for women in real estate. She meets a group of positive and supportive women who are also new to the industry. The women in the group offer each other support and encouragement. They also share tips and advice.

The woman starts to feel more confident about her abilities. She realizes that she is not alone and that there are other people who are there to support her. She also starts to believe in herself and in her ability to achieve her goals.

Surrounding herself with positive people has helped the woman to develop a winning mindset. She is now more motivated and focused on her goals. She is also more confident in her abilities. She is well on her way to success in the real estate industry.

If you want to develop a winning mindset, surround yourself with positive people. Positive people can help you to stay motivated, focused, and positive. They can also help you to overcome challenges and achieve your goals.

5. Visualize success: Visualization is a powerful tool that can help women develop a winning mindset in real estate. When women visualize success, they are programming their minds to believe that they can achieve their goals.

To visualize success, women should take some time each day to imagine themselves achieving their goals. They should see themselves as successful real estate agents or investors. They should imagine themselves closing deals, helping clients achieve their real estate dreams, and building a successful business.

The more women visualize success, the more likely they are to achieve it. Visualization helps to boost confidence, motivation, and focus. It also helps women to develop a clear vision of what they want to achieve.

Here are some tips for visualizing success in real estate:

1) Be specific. What do you want to achieve in your real estate career? Do you want to close a certain number of deals in a year? Do you want to invest in a certain number of properties? The more specific you are, the easier it will be to visualize your success.
2) Be positive. When you visualize success, see yourself achieving your goals with ease and confidence. Focus on the positive aspects of success, such as helping clients achieve their dreams and building a successful business.

3) Be consistent. Visualize success for a few minutes each day. The more consistent you are, the more powerful visualization will be.

Here is an example of how a woman can use visualization to develop a winning mindset in real estate:

A woman who is new to the real estate industry may have the goal of closing 10 deals in her first year. To visualize this goal, she can imagine herself closing a deal each month. She can imagine herself meeting with clients, showing them properties, and negotiating deals. She can also imagine herself celebrating her success with her colleagues and clients.

By visualizing success each day, the woman is programming her mind to believe that she can achieve her goal. She is also boosting her confidence and motivation. As a result, she is more likely to achieve her goal of closing 10 deals in her first year.

Visualization is a powerful tool that can help women to develop a winning mindset in real estate. By taking the time to visualize success, women can boost their confidence, motivation, focus, and clarity. As a result, they are more likely to achieve their goals and succeed in the real estate industry.

Here are some specific things that women can do to develop a winning mindset in real estate:

1. Challenge limiting beliefs. Many women have limiting beliefs about themselves and their abilities. These beliefs can hold them back from achieving their goals. It is important to challenge these beliefs and to replace them with positive beliefs.

2. Celebrate their successes. Women often downplay their successes or attribute them to luck. It is important for women to celebrate their successes and to give themselves credit for their accomplishments.

3. Network with other successful women in real estate. Networking with other successful women can help women to learn from each other, to share resources, and to support each other.

4. Find a mentor. A mentor can provide women with guidance, support, and advice. A mentor can also help women to connect with other people in the industry and to develop their skills and knowledge.

Developing a winning mindset takes time and effort, but it is worth it. A winning mindset can help women to achieve their goals, to overcome challenges, and to succeed in the real estate industry.

2.2. Overcoming self-doubt and limiting beliefs

Overcoming self-doubt and limiting beliefs is a crucial step for achieving success in any field, and it holds particular significance in the competitive and demanding world of real estate. Self-doubt and limiting beliefs can hinder one's potential, cloud judgment, and prevent individuals from taking the necessary risks and actions to achieve their goals.

What is Self-Doubt and Limiting Beliefs?

Self-doubt is a state of uncertainty or apprehension about one's abilities or worth. It can manifest as negative thoughts, such as "I'm not good enough" or "I'll never succeed in this industry." Limiting beliefs, on the other hand, are rigid and often irrational thoughts that restrict one's potential and prevent them from pursuing their goals. These beliefs often stem from past experiences or negative self-perceptions.

The Impact of Self-Doubt and Limiting Beliefs

Self-doubt and limiting beliefs can have a detrimental effect on one's performance in real estate. They can lead to procrastination, hesitation, and missed opportunities. These negative thoughts can also undermine confidence, making it difficult to connect with potential clients and negotiate effectively.

Overcoming Self-Doubt and Limiting Beliefs

Overcoming self-doubt and limiting beliefs is not an overnight process; it requires consistent effort and self-awareness. Here are some strategies for overcoming these challenges:

1. Identify Your Beliefs: Identifying self-doubt and limiting beliefs is a crucial step toward overcoming their negative influence on your life and achieving your goals. It's like clearing away the fog that obscures your true potential and hinders your progress. By recognizing these beliefs, you can begin to challenge their validity and replace them with empowering affirmations that foster a positive mindset and propel you forward.

The Importance of Identifying Beliefs

Self-doubt and limiting beliefs often operate subtly, embedded in our thoughts and influencing our actions without us fully realizing their impact. They can manifest as nagging insecurities, negative self-talk, or a hesitation to take risks. By identifying these beliefs, we bring them to light, making it possible to examine them critically and question their legitimacy.

How to Identify Self-Doubt and Limiting Beliefs

Identifying self-doubt and limiting beliefs requires introspection and self-awareness. Here are some effective strategies for uncovering these hidden obstacles:

a. Journaling: Dedicate time to journaling your thoughts and feelings. Observe patterns in your self-talk and identify recurring themes of doubt or negativity.

b. Seek Feedback: Ask trusted friends, mentors, or colleagues for their honest feedback on your strengths and areas for improvement. Their perspectives can help you gain valuable insights into your self-perceptions.

c. Analyze Past Experiences: Reflect on past experiences, both successes, and failures. Identify instances where self-doubt or limiting beliefs may have influenced your actions or outcomes.

d. Recognize Emotional Triggers: Pay attention to situations or interactions that trigger feelings of self-doubt or insecurity. These triggers can provide clues to underlying beliefs that need to be addressed.

e. Challenge Negative Thoughts: When negative thoughts arise, don't accept them at face value. Question their validity and consider alternative, more positive perspectives.

Examples of Self-Doubt and Limiting Beliefs

Here are some common examples of self-doubt and limiting beliefs that can hold women back in real estate:

- "I'm not good enough to compete in this industry."
- "I don't have the experience or knowledge to succeed."
- "I'll never be able to close as many deals as the top agents."

- "I'm not assertive enough to negotiate effectively."
- "I'm afraid of making mistakes and losing clients."
- Benefits of Identifying Self-Doubt and Limiting Beliefs

Identifying self-doubt and limiting beliefs offers several benefits:

a. Increased Self-Awareness: Gaining a deeper understanding of your beliefs empowers you to make informed decisions and take control of your thoughts and actions.

b. Challenged Negative Thoughts: By bringing limiting beliefs to light, you can challenge their validity and replace them with more positive and empowering affirmations.

c. Improved Decision-Making: With a clearer mind and a stronger sense of self-belief, you can make more confident and effective decisions in your real estate career.

d. Enhanced Performance: Overcoming self-doubt and limiting beliefs can lead to improved performance, increased productivity, and greater satisfaction in your work.

e. Achieved Goals: By removing these obstacles from your path, you'll find it easier to set and achieve your goals in real estate and other areas of your life.

Identifying self-doubt and limiting beliefs is not always easy, but it is an essential step toward personal growth and professional success. By taking the time to uncover these hidden barriers, you can empower yourself to break free from their grip and pursue your dreams with confidence and determination.

2. Challenge Your Beliefs: Self-doubt and limiting beliefs are like invisible chains that can hold us back from achieving our goals and living our best lives. They can whisper negative thoughts into our ears, making us question our abilities and preventing us from taking action. But we don't have to let these beliefs control us. We can challenge them, replace them with more positive thoughts, and step into the fullness of our potential.

What are Limiting Beliefs?

Limiting beliefs are rigid and often irrational thoughts that restrict our potential and prevent us from pursuing our goals. They are often based on past experiences or negative self-perceptions. For example, if you had a bad experience with a real estate agent in the past, you might develop a limiting belief that all real estate agents are dishonest. This limiting belief could prevent you from working with a real estate agent, even if you need one to buy or sell a home.

How to Challenge Your Limiting Beliefs

The first step to overcoming limiting beliefs is to identify them. What are the negative thoughts that are holding you back? Once you have identified your limiting beliefs, you can start to challenge them.

Here are some questions to ask yourself when challenging your limiting beliefs:

- Is this belief true?
- What evidence is there to support this belief?
- What would happen if I didn't believe this?
- What is the opposite of this belief?
- What would it be like if I believed the opposite of this belief?

By asking yourself these questions, you can start to see that your limiting beliefs are not necessarily true. They are just thoughts that you have been telling yourself for a long time.

Replacing Limiting Beliefs with Positive Affirmations

Once you have challenged your limiting beliefs, you can replace them with positive affirmations. Positive affirmations are statements that reinforce your strengths and capabilities. They can help you to believe in yourself and to overcome self-doubt.

Here are some examples of positive affirmations that you can use to replace limiting beliefs:

- I am capable of achieving my goals.
- I am confident in my abilities.
- I am worthy of success.
- I am a valuable asset to my clients.
- I am a successful real estate agent.
- Taking Action

In addition to challenging your limiting beliefs and replacing them with positive affirmations, it is also important to take action. The more you take action, the more confident you will become. And the more confident you become, the less you will be held back by self-doubt and limiting beliefs.

Here are some things you can do to take action:

- Set goals for yourself.
- Break down your goals into small steps.
- Take action on your goals, even if you're not feeling 100% confident.
- Celebrate your accomplishments along the way.

Remember, overcoming self-doubt and limiting beliefs is a journey, not a destination. There will be times when you feel discouraged, but don't give up. Just keep challenging your beliefs, replacing them with positive affirmations, and taking action. With time and effort, you will overcome your self-doubt and achieve your goals.

Challenging your beliefs is a powerful strategy for overcoming self-doubt and limiting beliefs. By identifying your limiting beliefs, questioning their validity, and replacing them with positive affirmations, you can empower yourself to achieve your full potential. Remember, you are capable of great things. Don't let self-doubt hold you back.

3. Replace Negative Thoughts with Positive Ones: Replacing negative thoughts with positive ones is a powerful strategy for overcoming self-doubt and limiting beliefs. Our thoughts have a profound impact on our emotions, behaviors, and ultimately, our success in various aspects of life, including real estate. Negative thoughts can undermine our confidence, hinder our decision-making, and prevent us from taking risks that lead to growth and achievement.

The practice of replacing negative thoughts with positive ones involves actively challenging and reframing our internal dialogue. It's about consciously choosing to focus on our strengths, past successes, and positive affirmations rather than dwelling on negative self-talk and limiting beliefs.

Identifying Negative Thoughts

The first step in this process is to identify and acknowledge negative thoughts when they arise. This can be challenging at first, as negative thoughts often become ingrained and automatic. However, paying attention to our inner dialogue and recognizing patterns of self-doubt is crucial for making a positive change.

Challenging Negative Thoughts

Once we've identified negative thoughts, we can begin to challenge their validity. Ask yourself if these thoughts are based on facts or if they are simply assumptions or fears. Often, negative thoughts are rooted in past experiences or societal stereotypes that may not accurately reflect our abilities or potential.

Replacing with Positive Affirmations

Instead of dwelling on negative thoughts, replace them with positive affirmations that reinforce your strengths, capabilities, and goals. These affirmations should be specific, realistic, and expressed in the present tense. For example, instead of thinking "I'm not good enough to succeed in real estate," replace it with "I am capable, knowledgeable, and have the skills to succeed in real estate."

Practicing Positive Self-Talk

Engage in regular positive self-talk throughout the day. Remind yourself of your accomplishments, celebrate your progress, and visualize yourself achieving your goals. Positive self-talk can help to rewire your neural pathways, making positive thoughts more natural and replacing negative ones over time.

Surrounding Yourself with Positivity

The environment you create for yourself plays a significant role in shaping your mindset. Surround yourself with supportive individuals who believe in your potential and encourage you to pursue your dreams. Limit exposure to negative influences that reinforce self-doubt and limiting beliefs.

Making it a Habit

Replacing negative thoughts with positive ones is an ongoing practice that requires consistent effort and self-awareness. It's not about suppressing negative thoughts completely, but rather about recognizing them, challenging their validity, and replacing them with positive affirmations.

The benefits of replacing negative thoughts with positive ones extend beyond overcoming self-doubt and limiting beliefs. Positive thinking can boost self-esteem, enhance creativity, improve problem-solving skills, and lead to greater resilience in the face of setbacks.

Replacing negative thoughts with positive ones can empower women to navigate the challenges of the industry with confidence, make informed decisions, and pursue their goals with unwavering determination. By cultivating a positive mindset, women can overcome self-doubt, break through limiting beliefs, and achieve success in this dynamic and rewarding field.

4. Seek Support: Overcoming self-doubt and limiting beliefs is a challenging endeavor that requires consistent effort and self-awareness. While self-reflection and positive affirmations can play a significant role in empowering oneself, seeking support from others can provide an invaluable external perspective and a sense of community that can significantly accelerate progress.

Benefits of Seeking Support

a. External Validation: Seeking support allows individuals to gain an objective perspective on their abilities and strengths. Feedback from trusted individuals can help challenge negative self-perceptions and reinforce positive self-beliefs.

b. Practical Advice: Experienced individuals or mentors can provide practical advice and guidance based on their own experiences and knowledge. This guidance can help individuals navigate challenges, develop strategies, and avoid common pitfalls.

c. Encouragement and Motivation: Knowing that others believe in your potential and are rooting for your success can provide a powerful source of encouragement and motivation. This support can help individuals persevere through setbacks and maintain their focus on their goals.

d. Sense of Community: Surrounding oneself with supportive individuals can create a sense of community and belonging. This sense of belonging can foster a more positive and optimistic mindset, making it easier to overcome self-doubt and limiting beliefs.

Specific Ways to Seek Support

a. Mentorship: Finding a mentor in the real estate industry can provide invaluable guidance and support. A mentor can share their expertise, offer advice on navigating challenges, and help connect you with other professionals in the field.

b. Professional Coaching: Seeking professional coaching can provide a structured approach to overcoming self-doubt and limiting beliefs. A coach can help you identify and challenge negative thought patterns, develop strategies for self-improvement, and set realistic goals.

c. Networking: Building relationships with other women in real estate can create a supportive network of peers who share similar experiences and challenges. Networking events, online forums, and professional organizations can provide opportunities to connect with like-minded individuals.

d. Support Groups: Joining a support group specifically for women in real estate can provide a safe and supportive environment to discuss challenges, share experiences, and receive encouragement from others who understand your unique perspective.

e. Therapy: If self-doubt and limiting beliefs are deeply ingrained or causing significant distress, seeking professional therapy can provide specialized support and guidance. A therapist can help you identify the root causes of these beliefs and develop effective coping mechanisms.

Overcoming self-doubt and limiting beliefs is not a solitary endeavor. Seeking support from mentors, coaches, peers, and professional counselors can provide the encouragement, guidance, and validation needed to achieve success in any field, including the competitive world of real estate.

5. Celebrate Achievements: Celebrating achievements is a powerful strategy for overcoming self-doubt and limiting beliefs. It reinforces self-belief, motivates continued effort, and enhances resilience in the face of challenges. By acknowledging and appreciating one's accomplishments, individuals can cultivate a positive mindset and build confidence in their abilities.

Celebrating achievements, regardless of their size or scale, serves as a reminder of one's capabilities and accomplishments. It shifts the focus away from perceived shortcomings and limitations, highlighting progress and growth. By recognizing and appreciating one's successes, individuals can counteract the negative impact of self-doubt and limiting beliefs.

Celebrating achievements has a profound impact on one's psychological state. It triggers the release of dopamine, a neurotransmitter associated with pleasure and reward. This positive reinforcement strengthens the neural pathways associated with success, making it easier to replicate these outcomes in the future.

To effectively celebrate achievements and reap their benefits, consider the following strategies:

1. Acknowledge and Reflect: Take time to acknowledge and reflect on your accomplishments. This involves recognizing the effort, skills, and perseverance that contributed to your success.
2. Share Your Achievements: Share your successes with supportive individuals who will genuinely celebrate your accomplishments. Their positive reinforcement can further boost your self-belief and motivation.
3. Document Your Achievements: Keep a record of your accomplishments, whether it's a physical journal or a digital portfolio. Revisiting this record can serve as a reminder of your capabilities and progress, especially during moments of self-doubt.
4. Reward Yourself: Celebrate your achievements with tangible rewards that bring you joy and satisfaction.

This reinforces the positive association with success and motivates continued effort.

Examples of Celebrating Achievements in Real Estate

For women in real estate, celebrating achievements can take on various forms:

- Completing a successful transaction: Recognize the hard work, expertise, and client satisfaction involved in closing a deal.
- Exceeding personal sales goals: Celebrate surpassing individual targets, demonstrating growth and achievement.
- Receiving positive client feedback: Acknowledge and appreciate positive comments from clients, validating your skills and service.
- Expanding your network: Celebrate building connections with potential clients, industry peers, and mentors.
- Learning new skills and knowledge: Recognize the effort and dedication invested in professional development.

Celebrating achievements is not about self-aggrandizement or boasting; it's about acknowledging one's growth, recognizing one's capabilities, and fostering a positive mindset that empowers individuals to pursue their goals with confidence and resilience. By embracing this practice, women in real estate can effectively combat self-doubt and limiting beliefs, paving the way for continued success and fulfillment in their chosen field.

In summary, overcoming self-doubt and limiting beliefs is a journey of self-discovery and growth. By recognizing these challenges, challenging negative thoughts, and replacing them with positive affirmations, women in real estate can empower themselves to achieve their full potential and succeed in this dynamic industry.

2.3. Building confidence and resilience

Confidence and resilience are essential qualities for success in any field, but they are particularly important in the competitive and demanding world of real estate. Confidence allows women to navigate the challenges of the industry, pursue opportunities with conviction, and build strong relationships with clients. Resilience enables them to overcome setbacks, adapt to changing market conditions, and persevere in the face of adversity.

Why Confidence and Resilience Are Crucial for Women in Real Estate

The real estate industry is a dynamic and complex environment, often characterized by uncertainty and competition. Women who possess confidence and resilience are better equipped to handle the challenges and setbacks that inevitably arise. They are able to:

1. Project a positive and professional image: Confidence instills trust and respect in clients, colleagues, and potential partners.

2. Negotiate effectively: Confidence allows women to advocate for themselves and their clients, achieving favorable terms in transactions.

3. Handle rejections: Resilience enables women to bounce back from disappointments and turn rejections into learning opportunities.

4. Adapt to change: The real estate market is constantly evolving, and resilient women can embrace new trends and technologies effectively.

Strategies for Building Confidence and Resilience

Developing confidence and resilience is an ongoing process that requires consistent effort and self-reflection. Here are some effective strategies for building these qualities:

1. Identify Strengths and Accomplishments: Regularly remind yourself of your strengths, skills, and past successes. This reinforces self-belief and boosts confidence.

2. Set Realistic Goals and Celebrate Achievements: Break down large goals into smaller, achievable steps. Celebrate each milestone, no matter how small, to reinforce a sense of progress and accomplishment.

3. Seek Feedback and Mentorship: Feedback from trusted mentors or colleagues can provide valuable insights and help identify areas for improvement.

4. Practice Positive Self-Talk: Replace negative thoughts with positive affirmations that emphasize your capabilities and potential.

5. Learn from Setbacks: View setbacks as learning opportunities and identify areas for improvement. Analyze what went wrong and develop strategies to avoid similar mistakes in the future.

6. Maintain a Healthy Work-Life Balance: Prioritize self-care and engage in activities that promote well-being. A healthy mind and body contribute to overall confidence and resilience.

7. Seek Support and Networking Opportunities: Surround yourself with supportive individuals who believe in your potential. Networking with successful women in real estate can provide inspiration and valuable guidance.

Resilience in Action: A Real-Life Example

Sarah, a relatively new real estate agent, faced a challenging situation when a potential client abruptly canceled a deal just before closing. Sarah could have easily succumbed to self-doubt and discouragement. However, she chose to focus on her resilience and took the following steps:

1. Analyzed the Situation: Sarah objectively reviewed the situation and identified factors that may have contributed to the client's decision.
2. Learned from the Experience: Sarah reflected on communication patterns and identified areas where she could improve client interactions.
3. Adapted Her Approach: Sarah refined her communication strategies, emphasizing proactive updates and addressing client concerns promptly.
4. Remained Positive: Sarah maintained a positive attitude and focused on her strengths and past successes.
5. Sought Support: Sarah discussed the situation with her mentor, who provided encouragement and valuable insights.

By demonstrating resilience, Sarah turned a setback into a learning opportunity and emerged stronger and more confident in her abilities.

In conclusion, building confidence and resilience is a continuous journey that requires dedication and self-awareness. Women in real estate who cultivate these qualities are better equipped to navigate the challenges of the industry, achieve their goals, and establish themselves as successful and respected professionals.

Chapter 3: Building a Strong Network in Real Estate

3.1. The importance of networking

Networking is the process of building and maintaining relationships with people to share information, exchange ideas, and gain access to opportunities. It is a crucial skill for success in any field, and it is especially important in real estate.

The real estate industry is a people-driven business, and networking allows you to build relationships with potential clients, lenders, brokers, and other professionals who can help you achieve your goals. Here are some specific reasons why networking is important in real estate:

1. Generate leads: Networking is a crucial aspect of success in the real estate industry, and one of its primary benefits is the ability to generate leads. By connecting with potential clients, lenders, brokers, and other professionals, you can expand your network and increase your chances of securing new business.

How Networking Generates Leads in Real Estate

a. Expanding Your Reach: Networking allows you to extend your reach beyond traditional marketing channels and connect with individuals who may not be actively searching for real estate services. By attending industry events, joining professional organizations, and participating in community activities, you can introduce yourself to a broader audience and establish relationships with potential clients.

b. Building Trust and Rapport: Networking is not just about exchanging information; it's about building relationships. By engaging in meaningful conversations, offering helpful advice, and demonstrating your expertise, you can gain the trust and rapport of potential clients. This trust can be instrumental in converting leads into actual transactions.

c. Gaining Referrals: Networking can lead to valuable referrals from satisfied clients, industry colleagues, and community members. These referrals carry significant weight as they come from trusted sources and often carry a positive perception of your services.

d. Identifying Market Needs: Networking provides a direct channel to understand the specific needs and desires of potential clients. By interacting with individuals at different stages of the homebuying or selling process, you can gain valuable insights into market trends and tailor your services accordingly.

e. Staying Top of Mind: Consistent networking helps you stay visible and top of mind among potential clients. Regular interactions, even if not directly related to business, can keep your name and services fresh in their minds when they are ready to make a real estate decision.

Strategies for Generating Leads Through Networking

a. Active Participation: Actively participate in industry events, professional organizations, and community activities. Introduce yourself, engage in conversations, and make a positive impression.

b. Value-Added Interactions: Offer valuable insights, share your expertise, and provide helpful advice. Position yourself as a trusted resource and demonstrate your commitment to helping others.

c. Strategic Connections: Identify and connect with key individuals in your network, such as lenders, brokers, and community leaders. These connections can provide valuable referrals and expand your reach.

d. Follow-up and Nurturing: Follow up with new connections promptly and maintain regular communication. Nurture these relationships by providing ongoing value and staying in touch with their needs.

e. Leverage Online Networking: Utilize social media platforms like LinkedIn and Facebook to connect with potential clients and industry professionals. Engage in relevant discussions, share informative content, and build your online presence.

f. Seek Referrals: Proactively seek referrals from satisfied clients, industry partners, and community members. Encourage them to recommend your services to their network.

g. Host Events or Workshops: Host informative events, workshops, or seminars related to real estate. These events can attract potential clients, showcase your expertise, and generate new leads.

h. Engage in Local Partnerships: Partner with local businesses, community organizations, or neighborhood groups. Cross-promote services and provide joint offerings to expand your reach and generate leads.

i. Utilize Customer Relationship Management (CRM) Tools: Employ CRM tools to organize your network, track interactions, and manage leads effectively.

j. Continuously Refine Your Approach: Regularly evaluate your networking strategies and identify areas for improvement. Adapt your approach based on your experiences and market trends.

By actively networking, providing value, and building genuine relationships, you can effectively generate leads and expand your client base in the competitive real estate industry. Remember, networking is a long-term investment that yields significant returns over time.

2. Gain knowledge and insights: Networking is a critical aspect of success in the real estate industry, providing a wealth of opportunities to expand knowledge and gain valuable insights. By connecting with experienced professionals and engaging in meaningful conversations, real estate agents and brokers can stay abreast of the latest trends, strategies, and market dynamics, enabling them to make informed decisions and enhance their expertise.

Networking provides direct access to real-time market information and insights from industry insiders. Through discussions with experienced brokers, appraisers, and investors, real estate professionals can gain a deeper understanding of current market conditions, emerging trends, and potential opportunities. This insider knowledge can be instrumental in identifying promising deals, making informed pricing decisions, and effectively navigating the ever-changing real estate landscape.

Networking provides a platform to learn from experienced professionals who have a wealth of knowledge and expertise to share. By engaging with seasoned brokers and agents, real estate professionals can gain valuable insights into negotiation strategies, marketing techniques, and client relationship management. This mentorship can accelerate their professional development and help them refine their skills to achieve greater success.

The real estate industry is constantly evolving, with new regulations and policies emerging regularly. Networking allows real estate professionals to stay up-to-date on these changes, ensuring that they are compliant with legal requirements and can effectively guide their clients through the complexities of the regulatory landscape. This knowledge can protect them from potential liabilities and enhance their reputation as trusted advisors.

Networking can open doors to new and lucrative investment opportunities. By connecting with investors and developers, real estate professionals can gain access to off-market properties, pre-development deals, and exclusive investment opportunities. This insider access can significantly enhance their ability to generate leads and secure profitable deals for their clients.

Networking expands a real estate professional's network of colleagues, mentors, and potential clients. This broader network can provide support, guidance, and referrals, which can be invaluable in navigating the challenges and opportunities of the real estate market. Additionally, networking can lead to access to specialized resources, such as property management services, legal counsel, and financing options.

Networking, therefore, is not merely about building relationships; it is about gaining access to a treasure trove of knowledge, insights, and opportunities that can propel real estate professionals to greater success. By actively engaging with their peers, seeking mentorship, and staying informed about industry trends, real estate professionals can elevate their expertise and make a lasting impact in the dynamic world of real estate.

3. Build credibility and reputation:

Building credibility and reputation is one of the most important reasons why networking is essential in real estate. A strong reputation can open doors to new opportunities, attract more clients, and help you command higher fees. In the competitive world of real estate, a positive reputation can be your most valuable asset.

Credibility and reputation are essential for success in real estate because they establish trust with potential clients and business partners. When you have a strong reputation, people are more likely to do business with you because they know you are reliable, knowledgeable, and trustworthy.

Networking provides several opportunities to build credibility and reputation in real estate. Here are some specific ways in which networking can help:

1. Establish relationships with key players: By connecting with experienced brokers, lenders, and other professionals in the industry, you can gain valuable insights and establish yourself as a credible member of the real estate community.
2. Receive referrals and recommendations: Networking can lead to referrals and recommendations from satisfied clients and colleagues. Positive word-of-mouth is a powerful marketing tool in real estate, and networking can help you generate more leads and close more deals.
3. Demonstrate expertise and knowledge: Participating in industry events, contributing to online forums, and sharing your knowledge with others can showcase your expertise and establish you as a thought leader in the real estate field.

4. Build a positive image: Networking allows you to interact with people in a professional setting, demonstrating your communication skills, interpersonal abilities, and commitment to ethical practices. This can help you build a positive image and enhance your reputation.

Strategies for Building Credibility and Reputation Through Networking

Here are some specific strategies for building credibility and reputation through networking in real estate:

1. Be a valuable resource: Offer your help and expertise to others, whether it's providing market insights, sharing tips on navigating the buying or selling process, or connecting them with relevant professionals.
2. Actively participate in industry organizations: Get involved in local and national real estate organizations, attend their events, and volunteer for committees or leadership positions. This shows your dedication to the industry and willingness to contribute.
3. Seek opportunities to mentor or teach: Share your knowledge and experience by mentoring new real estate agents or conducting workshops or seminars. This positions you as an expert and helps others in the industry.
4. Maintain an active online presence: Engage in online real estate forums, participate in relevant social media groups, and create informative blog posts or videos. This demonstrates your expertise and keeps you visible in the online space.
5. Consistently deliver exceptional service: Provide exceptional service to every client, no matter the size or

complexity of the deal. Positive experiences with clients will lead to referrals, testimonials, and a strong reputation.

Remember, building credibility and reputation takes time and consistent effort. By actively networking, demonstrating your expertise, and providing exceptional service, you can establish yourself as a trusted and respected professional in the real estate industry.

4. Access to opportunities: Networking in the real estate industry can open doors to numerous opportunities, expanding your professional reach and propelling your career forward. Here are some specific ways in which networking can provide access to opportunities in real estate:

a. Generating Leads and Expanding Clientele: Networking provides a direct channel to connect with potential clients, expanding your market reach and fostering new business relationships. By actively engaging with industry professionals, attending events, and participating in online forums, you can introduce yourself to a broader audience of individuals seeking real estate services.

b. Securing Partnerships and Collaborations: Networking can lead to fruitful partnerships and collaborations with other real estate agents, brokers, and investors. These partnerships can provide access to a wider range of properties, expertise, and resources, enabling you to expand your service offerings and reach a broader client base.

c. Gaining Insights and Market Knowledge: Networking allows you to tap into the collective wisdom and experience of seasoned professionals in the real estate industry. By connecting with established agents, brokers, and investors, you can gain valuable insights into market trends, emerging opportunities, and strategies for navigating the complexities of the real estate market.

d. Unearthing Off-Market Properties: Networking can unveil hidden gems in the real estate market – off-market properties that are not publicly listed. By cultivating relationships with brokers, agents, and investors, you may gain access to exclusive properties that are not readily available to the general public, giving you a competitive edge in securing desirable listings for your clients.

e. Attracting Investors and Financial Backing: Networking can open doors to potential investors who are seeking opportunities in the real estate market. By establishing connections with investment firms, private lenders, and individuals seeking real estate investments, you can showcase your expertise, attract funding for your projects, and expand your investment portfolio

f. Enhancing Personal Branding and Reputation: Active networking elevates your visibility and establishes your reputation as a trusted and knowledgeable real estate professional. By engaging in meaningful interactions, providing valuable insights, and consistently demonstrating your expertise, you build a strong personal brand that attracts clients, partners, and investors.

g. Discovering New Career Paths and Opportunities: Networking can reveal unexplored career paths and opportunities within the real estate industry. By connecting with professionals in various specializations, you may discover new areas of interest, explore niche markets, and identify opportunities to expand your skill set and career trajectory.

In essence, networking in real estate is akin to unlocking a treasure trove of opportunities. It empowers you to expand your professional network, gain access to exclusive deals, secure partnerships, attract investors, and elevate your career to new heights. Embrace the power of networking and watch your real estate business flourish.

Networking is an essential skill for success in real estate. By building and maintaining relationships with other professionals, you can generate leads, gain knowledge, build credibility, and access new opportunities.

3.2. How to identify and connect with key people in the real estate industry

Building a strong network is crucial for success in the real estate industry. By connecting with key people, you can gain access to valuable information, insights, and opportunities that can help you advance your career and achieve your goals.

Identifying Key People in Real Estate

Key people in the real estate industry include:

1. Potential clients: These are individuals or families who are looking to buy or sell a home, invest in real estate, or rent a property. Identifying potential clients requires understanding their needs, preferences, and budget.

2. Lenders: Lenders provide financing for real estate transactions. Connecting with lenders can help you secure mortgages for your clients and expand your business opportunities.

3. Brokers: Brokers act as intermediaries between buyers and sellers, facilitating real estate transactions. Networking with

brokers can increase your exposure to potential clients and deals.

4. Appraisers: Appraisers assess the value of properties, ensuring fair transactions. Connecting with appraisers can enhance your knowledge of market values and provide insights for your clients.

5. Title companies: Title companies handle the legal aspects of real estate transactions, ensuring title transfers and protecting property rights. Networking with title companies can streamline your transactions and protect your clients' interests.

6. Industry experts: Industry experts, such as real estate attorneys, tax advisors, and property managers, provide specialized services that can benefit your clients. Connecting with these experts can enhance your knowledge and expand your network's capabilities.

Connecting with Key People in Real Estate

Once you have identified key people in the real estate industry, there are several effective strategies to connect with them:

1. Attend industry events: Attending industry events is a highly effective strategy for connecting with key people in the real estate industry. These events provide a concentrated opportunity to meet and interact with a diverse group of professionals, including potential clients, lenders, brokers, appraisers, title company representatives, industry experts, and fellow agents.

Types of Industry Events

The real estate industry offers a variety of events, each catering to specific interests and goals. Here are some common types of industry events:

a. Conferences: Large-scale conferences bring together hundreds or even thousands of real estate professionals from across the country or even internationally. These events typically feature keynote speakers, breakout sessions, networking receptions, and exhibition halls showcasing the latest products and services.

b. Seminars: Smaller and more focused seminars delve into specific topics or trends in real estate. They often feature expert speakers and provide in-depth discussions and case studies.

c. Workshops: Workshops provide hands-on training and practical skills development in various aspects of real estate, such as marketing, negotiation, or technology.

d. Networking Events: Social gatherings and networking receptions offer a relaxed atmosphere to connect with fellow professionals, exchange business cards, and build relationships.

Benefits of Attending Industry Events

Attending industry events provides numerous benefits for real estate professionals:

a. Expand your network: Industry events are a goldmine for expanding your network. You can meet a wide range of professionals in a short period, making valuable connections that can benefit your business.

b. Gain knowledge and insights: Industry events often feature expert speakers and presentations that provide valuable insights into the latest market trends, regulations, and strategies.

c. Stay ahead of the curve: Keep abreast of emerging trends and technologies in the real estate industry by attending events that focus on innovation and advancements.

d. Enhance your reputation: Participating in industry events demonstrates your commitment to professional development and can enhance your reputation among colleagues and potential clients.

e. Generate leads and business opportunities: Networking at industry events can lead to direct referrals, partnerships, and new business opportunities.

Strategies for Maximizing Networking at Industry Events

To make the most of industry events and maximize your networking opportunities, consider these strategies:

a. Set goals: Before attending an event, define your goals for networking. Are you looking to connect with potential clients, expand your referral network, or learn about new technologies? Having clear goals will help you focus your efforts.

b. Prepare a well-crafted introduction: Develop a concise and memorable introduction that highlights your expertise, experience, and value proposition. Practice your introduction to deliver it confidently and professionally.

c. Bring business cards: Have plenty of business cards on hand to exchange with potential connections. Consider including a personalized note or QR code linking to your website or social media profiles.

d. Actively participate: Engage in conversations, ask thoughtful questions, and share your insights. Show active interest in the discussions and the people you encounter.

e. Follow up: After the event, follow up with promising connections via email or LinkedIn. Send a personalized message reminding them of your conversation and reiterating your interest in staying connected or exploring potential opportunities.

Attending industry events is a strategic investment in your real estate career. By actively networking, learning from experts, and staying up-to-date with trends, you can expand your professional circle, generate new business opportunities, and position yourself for success in the dynamic real estate market.

2. Join professional organizations: Joining professional organizations is a highly effective strategy for connecting with key people in the real estate industry. These organizations provide a valuable platform for networking, learning, and staying up-to-date on the latest trends and developments in the field.

Benefits of Joining Professional Organizations in Real Estate

a. Networking Opportunities: Professional organizations offer numerous opportunities to connect with other real estate professionals, including potential clients, lenders, brokers, appraisers, and industry experts. These connections can lead to valuable referrals, partnerships, and business opportunities.

b. Educational Resources: Professional organizations provide access to a wealth of educational resources, such as seminars, conferences, and online courses. These resources can help you stay up-to-date on the latest industry trends, regulations, and best practices.

c. Professional Development: Professional organizations offer various opportunities for professional development, such as certifications, mentorship programs, and leadership training. These opportunities can help you enhance your skills, knowledge, and credibility in the real estate industry.

d. Industry Advocacy: Professional organizations advocate for the interests of real estate professionals and the industry as a whole. By joining, you can contribute to shaping policies and regulations that affect your business and the industry's future.

e. Career Advancement: Professional organizations can play a significant role in advancing your career. By actively participating in events, committees, and leadership roles, you can gain visibility, build relationships, and open doors to new opportunities.

Specific Examples of Professional Organizations in Real Estate

a. National Association of Realtors (NAR): NAR is the largest real estate trade organization in the United States, representing over 1.5 million real estate professionals. It offers a wide range of resources, including networking events, educational programs, and advocacy initiatives.

b. National Association of Real Estate Brokers (NAREB): NAREB is the oldest and largest trade organization for African-American real estate professionals. It provides a platform for networking, education, and advocacy for its members.

c. Commercial Real Estate Development Association (NAIOP): NAIOP is a leading organization for commercial real estate professionals, providing networking opportunities, educational resources, and industry advocacy.

d. International Council of Shopping Centers (ICSC): ICSC is a global organization for retail and real estate professionals, offering networking events, educational programs, and industry research.

e. Women's Council of REALTORS® (WCR): WCR is a network for women in the real estate industry, providing support, resources, and advocacy for its members.

Strategies for Effective Networking within Professional Organizations

a. Attend events and meetings: Actively participate in events organized by the professional organization. These events provide opportunities to meet new people, make introductions, and build relationships.

b. Join committees and task forces: Volunteer to participate in committees and task forces related to your areas of expertise. This demonstrates your interest in the organization and provides opportunities to collaborate with other professionals.

c. Mentor and be mentored: Seek out mentorship opportunities from experienced professionals in the organization. Conversely, offer mentorship to those less experienced, sharing your knowledge and insights.

d. Build relationships with key people: Identify individuals within the organization who can be valuable connections. Focus on building genuine relationships with these individuals, offering support and assistance when possible.

e. Engage online: Utilize the organization's online platforms, such as discussion forums and social media groups, to connect with members and share your expertise.

By actively participating in professional organizations, you can expand your network, enhance your knowledge, and advance your career in the real estate industry. These organizations provide a supportive environment for professional growth and can open doors to new opportunities and collaborations.

3. Leverage social media: Social media has become an indispensable tool for networking and connecting with key people in the real estate industry. With its vast reach and diverse user base, social media platforms offer a unique opportunity to expand your network, build relationships, and generate leads. Here's how to effectively leverage social media to connect with key people in real estate:

a. Choose the Right Platforms: Focus on social media platforms that align with your target audience and industry trends. LinkedIn is a popular choice for professional networking, while Facebook and Instagram are ideal for building brand awareness and reaching a wider audience.

b. Create a Professional Profile: Craft a compelling profile that highlights your expertise, experience, and accomplishments in the real estate industry. Use high-quality images, a clear bio, and relevant keywords to make your profile easily searchable.

c. Engage with Industry Groups and Discussions: Join relevant real estate groups and forums on social media. Actively participate in discussions, share your insights, and provide valuable contributions to establish yourself as a thought leader.

d. Connect with Key Individuals: Search for real estate professionals, potential clients, lenders, and other key players in your network. Send personalized invitations, engage with their content, and offer congratulations on their achievements.

e. Share Industry News and Insights: Regularly share relevant news, articles, and updates from the real estate industry. This showcases your knowledge and positions you as a trusted source of information.

f. Showcase Your Work: Share success stories, case studies, and positive client testimonials to demonstrate your expertise and attract potential clients.

g. Utilize Social Media Advertising: Consider running targeted social media ads to reach a wider audience and connect with potential clients who may not be actively seeking real estate services.

h. Track Your Results: Use social media analytics to track your engagement, reach, and lead generation efforts. This will help you refine your strategies and optimize your social media presence.

Here are some additional tips for leveraging social media effectively:

- Be consistent: Regular posting and engagement are crucial for maintaining visibility and staying top-of-mind with your network.
- Be authentic: Let your personality shine through and avoid overly promotional or robotic content.
- Be respectful: Social media is a public forum, so be mindful of your interactions and avoid negativity or inappropriate behavior.

- Be patient: Building relationships and generating leads takes time and effort. Stay committed to your social media strategy and nurture the connections you make.

By leveraging social media strategically, you can expand your network, connect with key people in the real estate industry, and position yourself as a trusted expert, leading to more opportunities and success in your career.

4. Get involved in your community: Networking is a crucial aspect of success in the real estate industry, and it goes beyond attending industry events or joining professional organizations. Getting involved in your community is an effective strategy to connect with key people in the real estate industry, build strong relationships, and generate leads.

Why Get Involved in Your Community

Engaging in your community provides several benefits for real estate professionals:

a. Visibility and Credibility: Active participation in community events, volunteer organizations, and local business groups increases your visibility among potential clients, lenders, and other key players in the area. This exposure helps establish your credibility and reputation as a trusted and involved member of the community.

b. Building Relationships: Volunteering your time and expertise to community initiatives creates opportunities to interact with potential clients, lenders, and other professionals in a relaxed and non-transactional setting. These interactions foster genuine connections and lay the foundation for future business opportunities.

c. Local Market Insights: By immersing yourself in community activities, you gain valuable insights into the local neighborhoods, demographics, and market trends. This knowledge enhances your ability to serve your clients effectively and position yourself as an expert in the area.

d. Referrals and Recommendations: Community involvement can lead to referrals and recommendations from satisfied residents, business owners, and community leaders. These referrals can be a powerful source of new leads and business opportunities.

e. Positive Brand Image: Actively participating in community initiatives helps create a positive image for your real estate business. It demonstrates your commitment to the community and your willingness to go beyond simply selling properties.

Strategies for Getting Involved in Your Community

There are numerous ways to get involved in your community, depending on your interests and availability. Here are some effective strategies:

a. Volunteer for Local Organizations: Identify local organizations that align with your values and interests, such as youth programs, environmental groups, or community development initiatives. Offer your time, skills, or expertise to support their causes.

b. Join Local Business Groups: Participate in chambers of commerce, business networking groups, or industry associations in your area. These groups provide opportunities to connect with other professionals, stay informed about local business developments, and promote your expertise.

c. Attend Community Events: Attend neighborhood fairs, festivals, sports tournaments, or cultural events. These events provide opportunities to mingle with potential clients, introduce yourself to community leaders, and showcase your involvement in the area.

d. Support Local Businesses: Patronize local businesses, attend their events, and promote their products or services. Building relationships with local business owners can lead to referrals, partnerships, and a stronger connection to the community.

e. Get Involved in Local Government: Attend town hall meetings, participate in civic planning initiatives, or volunteer for community boards or committees. This involvement demonstrates your commitment to the community and can provide valuable insights into local development plans.

Maximizing the Impact of Community Involvement

To maximize the impact of your community involvement, consider these tips:

- Be Genuine and Enthusiastic: Show genuine interest in the community and the organizations you support. Your enthusiasm will be contagious and make you a more approachable and memorable connection.
- Be a Consistent Presence: Regular participation in community events and initiatives demonstrates your commitment and strengthens your relationships with other community members.
- Use social media to Amplify Your Involvement: Share your community involvement on social media platforms to increase visibility and inspire others to participate.
- Leverage Your Network: Inform your existing clients, colleagues, and referral partners about your community

involvement. This can lead to additional referrals and opportunities.

- Seek Opportunities to Help: Actively seek opportunities to utilize your real estate expertise to assist community organizations or local businesses. This will showcase your value and enhance your reputation.

By getting involved in your community, you not only contribute to its betterment but also expand your network, build strong relationships, and generate new business opportunities. This strategy is a win-win for both the community and your real estate career.

5. Referrals: Referrals are one of the most effective strategies for connecting with key people in the real estate industry. They provide a warm introduction to potential clients, lenders, brokers, and other professionals who may be interested in your services or expertise.

Referrals hold significant power in the real estate industry for several reasons:

- Credibility: Referrals come from satisfied clients or trusted colleagues, adding a layer of credibility and trust to your introduction. Potential clients are more likely to engage with you when they have a positive recommendation from someone they know and respect.
- Warm Introduction: Referrals create a warm introduction, breaking the ice and establishing a connection before you even meet. This can make it easier to build rapport, discuss their needs, and present your services effectively.
- Targeted Networking: Referrals allow you to target specific individuals or groups that align with your

expertise and potential clients. This focused approach increases the likelihood of successful connections and business opportunities.

To effectively generate referrals in the real estate industry, consider the following strategies:

a. Exceptional Client Service: Deliver outstanding service to every client, exceeding their expectations and building strong relationships. Satisfied clients are more likely to refer you to their friends and family.

b. Ask for Referrals: Don't hesitate to ask for referrals directly from your clients. Express your appreciation for their business and politely request the opportunity to assist their network.

c. Nurture Relationships: Stay in touch with past clients, sending periodic updates, market insights, or holiday greetings. Maintaining these connections can lead to future referrals and repeat business.

d. Network with Industry Professionals: Build relationships with other real estate professionals, such as lenders, brokers, and appraisers. Referrals from colleagues can expand your reach and introduce you to new clients.

e. Engage in Community Activities: Participate in local events, volunteer organizations, and community groups. This can increase your visibility, build rapport with potential clients, and generate referral opportunities.

f. Leverage Online Platforms: Utilize online platforms like LinkedIn and Facebook to connect with real estate professionals and potential clients. Share relevant content, engage in discussions, and seek referrals from your online network.

g. Offer Incentives: Consider offering incentives for referrals, such as gift cards, discounts, or even a portion of your commission. This can motivate clients to refer to their network and encourage repeat business.

Once you receive a referral, take steps to maximize its impact:

- Express Gratitude: Thank the client for the referral and acknowledge their trust in your services.
- Prompt Response: Respond promptly to the referral, showing your commitment to their needs and building confidence in your professionalism.
- Thorough Preparation: Before meeting the referral, gather relevant information about their needs, preferences, and budget. This demonstrates your dedication and increases the likelihood of a successful transaction.
- Maintain Communication: Keep both the client and the referral updated throughout the process, ensuring transparency and fostering trust.
- Seek Feedback: After closing the deal, seek feedback from both the client and the referral. This valuable input can help you improve your services and refine your referral strategy.

By consistently delivering exceptional service, actively seeking referrals, and nurturing relationships, you can cultivate a network of satisfied clients and industry professionals who will advocate for your services and contribute to your success in the real estate industry.

By identifying and connecting with key people in the real estate industry, building strong relationships, and providing consistent value, you can create a powerful network that will support your growth and success in this dynamic field.

3.3. Building and maintaining relationships

Building and maintaining relationships is the cornerstone of success in any industry, and real estate is no exception. In this competitive and people-driven business, strong relationships with clients, colleagues, and industry partners can open doors to new opportunities, generate leads, and foster a positive reputation.

The Importance of Building Relationships in Real Estate

Relationships are the foundation of trust and loyalty, which are essential elements for success in real estate. By building strong relationships with your clients, you can:

1. Gain their trust and confidence: When clients trust you, they are more likely to rely on your expertise, recommend you to others, and return for future business.

2. Understand their needs and preferences: Building a rapport with clients allows you to understand their specific needs, wants, and concerns, enabling you to provide personalized and effective service.

3. Anticipate their expectations: By understanding your clients' expectations, you can proactively address their concerns and exceed their expectations, leading to greater satisfaction and loyalty.

Effective Strategies for Building Relationships in Real Estate

Building strong relationships in real estate requires consistent effort, genuine care, and a focus on providing value. Here are some effective strategies to consider:

1. Active listening: Show your clients that you value their input by actively listening to their needs, concerns, and aspirations.

2. Effective communication: Communicate regularly with your clients, providing updates on the progress of their transactions, addressing any questions or concerns promptly, and keeping them informed throughout the process.

3. Exceeding expectations: Go above and beyond to exceed your clients' expectations by anticipating their needs, offering helpful suggestions, and going the extra mile to ensure their satisfaction.

4. Staying in touch: Maintain regular communication with your clients even after closing a deal. Send birthday greetings, holiday cards, or market updates to keep them informed and engaged.

5. Networking with colleagues: Develop strong relationships with fellow real estate professionals, including brokers, lenders, appraisers, and title agents. These connections can provide valuable referrals, insights, and support.

6. Involvement in professional organizations: Engage with local and national real estate organizations, such as the National Association of Realtors (NAR) or the National Association of Real Estate Brokers (NAREB). These organizations provide networking opportunities, educational resources, and a platform to connect with industry leaders.

Maintaining Relationships in Real Estate

Building relationships is just the beginning; maintaining them requires ongoing effort and dedication. Here are some key practices for maintaining strong relationships in real estate:

1. Stay consistent: Maintain consistent communication and interaction with your clients, even after the transaction is complete. Regular check-ins and updates demonstrate your commitment to their satisfaction.

2. Provide ongoing value: Continuously offer value to your clients by sharing market updates, providing helpful tips, and offering assistance with any real estate-related needs they may have.

3. Show appreciation: Express gratitude to your clients for their business and referrals. A handwritten thank-you note, a small gift, or a personalized message can go a long way in strengthening the relationship.

4. Be a resource: Become a trusted resource for your clients by staying up-to-date on real estate trends, regulations, and market conditions. Share your knowledge and insights to establish yourself as a valuable expert in their eyes.

5. Celebrate their successes: Congratulate your clients on their milestones, such as buying their first home, investing in a property, or achieving their real estate goals. Recognizing their achievements demonstrates your genuine care and support.

By building and maintaining strong relationships with clients, colleagues, and industry partners, you can create a network of support, generate leads, and establish a reputation as a trusted and reliable real estate professional. These connections will not only contribute to your success in the industry but also foster a sense of community and camaraderie within the real estate landscape.

Chapter 4: Marketing Yourself as a Successful Woman in Real Estate

4.1. Creating a strong personal brand

In the competitive world of real estate, creating a strong personal brand is essential for establishing yourself as a trusted and sought-after professional. A strong personal brand differentiates you from the crowd, attracts potential clients, and enhances your credibility in the industry.

What is a Personal Brand?

A personal brand is the unique image and reputation you create for yourself in the real estate industry. It encompasses your expertise, values, personality, and overall professional identity. A strong personal brand resonates with your target audience, sets you apart from competitors, and establishes you as a thought leader in your field.

Why is Personal Branding Important for Women in Real Estate?

Women in real estate face unique challenges in establishing their presence and gaining recognition. Personal branding empowers women to overcome these challenges and position themselves as successful professionals. By creating a strong personal brand, women can:

1. Stand out from the crowd: In a competitive industry, a strong personal brand helps women differentiate themselves from other real estate agents. It allows them to showcase their unique expertise, values, and personality, making them more memorable and appealing to potential clients.

2. Build trust and credibility: A well-crafted personal brand establishes trust and credibility among clients, colleagues, and

industry peers. By consistently demonstrating their expertise, professionalism, and commitment to client satisfaction, women can build a strong reputation that attracts new business and fosters lasting relationships.

3. Attract potential clients: A strong personal brand acts as a magnet for potential clients. By establishing a clear and consistent online presence, engaging with the community, and sharing valuable insights, women can attract clients who resonate with their brand and seek their services.

4. Position themselves as thought leaders: By consistently sharing their knowledge and expertise, women can establish themselves as thought leaders in the real estate industry. This can lead to speaking engagements, media appearances, and opportunities to influence industry trends.

Creating a Strong Personal Brand

Creating a strong personal brand requires a strategic and consistent approach. Here are some key steps to consider:

1. Define your brand identity: Start by defining your core values, expertise, and target audience. What makes you unique as a real estate professional? What are your passions and areas of specialization? Identifying your brand identity will guide your branding efforts.

2. Craft a compelling brand message: Develop a clear and concise brand message that articulates your value proposition to potential clients. What makes you the best choice for their real estate needs? Highlight your unique skills, experience, and approach to real estate.

3. Establish a consistent online presence: Create a professional website that showcases your expertise, services, and client

testimonials. Utilize social media platforms to engage with potential clients, share industry insights, and promote your brand.

4. Get involved in the community: Participate in local events, join professional organizations, and network with other real estate professionals. This will help you increase your visibility, build relationships, and establish yourself as a trusted member of the community.

5. Demonstrate your expertise: Share your knowledge and insights through blog posts, articles, social media content, or webinars. This will establish you as a thought leader in the industry and attract potential clients seeking your expertise.

6. Seek feedback and refine your brand: Regularly evaluate your branding efforts and seek feedback from colleagues, clients, and mentors. Use this feedback to refine your brand message, content, and overall approach to personal branding.

By following these steps and consistently demonstrating your expertise, professionalism, and commitment to client satisfaction, you can create a strong personal brand that will set you apart as a successful woman in the real estate industry. Remember, personal branding is an ongoing process that requires dedication and consistency. By investing in your brand, you are investing in your future success in the competitive world of real estate.

4.2. Developing a powerful online presence

In today's digital age, developing a powerful online presence has become essential for success in any field, and it holds particular significance for women in the real estate industry. A strong online presence can help women in real estate attract potential clients, showcase their expertise, and establish themselves as credible and trustworthy professionals.

What is an Online Presence?

An online presence refers to the digital footprint an individual or organization leaves across the internet. It encompasses various aspects, including:

1. A professional website: A well-designed and informative website serves as the foundation of an online presence. It should highlight your expertise, services, and contact information, making it easy for potential clients to find and learn about you.

2. Social media engagement: Active participation on social media platforms like LinkedIn, Facebook, and Instagram can expand your reach, connect with potential clients, and establish your brand as a thought leader in the industry.

3. Content creation: Sharing valuable and informative content, such as blog posts, videos, and infographics, demonstrates your knowledge and expertise, attracting potential clients and establishing your credibility.

4. Online reviews and testimonials: Positive online reviews and testimonials from satisfied clients can significantly enhance your online reputation and boost your credibility.

Why is an Online Presence Important for Women in Real Estate?

A strong online presence can empower women in real estate to:

1. Attract potential clients: A well-crafted online presence can increase your visibility and attract potential clients who are actively searching for real estate services online.

2. Showcase expertise: Creating informative content and engaging in industry discussions establishes your expertise and positions you as a trusted advisor in the real estate market.

3. Build credibility: Positive online reviews, testimonials, and industry recognition enhance your credibility and make you a more attractive choice for potential clients.

4. Establish a strong brand: A consistent and professional online presence helps you create a recognizable brand that differentiates you from competitors and leaves a lasting impression on potential clients.

How to Develop a Powerful Online Presence as a Woman in Real Estate

Here are some effective strategies for developing a powerful online presence as a woman in real estate:

1. Create a professional website: Invest in a well-designed and informative website that showcases your expertise, services, and contact information. Ensure it is mobile-friendly and optimized for search engines.

2. Engage actively on social media: Select relevant social media platforms and maintain an active presence. Share valuable content, engage with followers, and participate in industry discussions to expand your reach.

3. Become a content creator: Regularly create informative and engaging content, such as blog posts, videos, and infographics, to establish your thought leadership and attract potential clients.

4. Encourage online reviews: Encourage satisfied clients to leave positive reviews on relevant platforms like Google My Business and Zillow. Testimonials can significantly enhance your credibility and attract new clients.

5. Network online: Connect with other real estate professionals, potential clients, and industry influencers through social media and online communities. Building a strong online network can open doors to new opportunities.

In addition to these strategies, here are some specific tips for women in real estate to enhance their online presence:

Highlight your unique value proposition: Clearly articulate what sets you apart from other real estate professionals, emphasizing your strengths, experience, and commitment to serving clients.

1. Showcase your personality: Let your personality shine through your online interactions. Be authentic, approachable, and passionate about your work.
2. Use visuals effectively: Utilize high-quality images and videos to capture attention and make your content more engaging.
3. Respond promptly to inquiries: Respond promptly to messages, comments, and inquiries on social media and your website. This demonstrates professionalism and commitment to client service.
4. Monitor your online reputation: Regularly check online reviews, mentions, and discussions related to your name and services. Address any negative feedback promptly and professionally.

By implementing these strategies and cultivating a strong online presence, women in real estate can effectively attract potential clients, establish their expertise, and achieve success in this competitive industry. Remember, an online presence is an ongoing process that requires consistent effort and adaptation to the ever-evolving digital landscape.

4.3. Networking and marketing offline

Networking and marketing offline are essential strategies for women in real estate to establish a strong presence, build relationships, and attract potential clients. While online marketing has become a dominant force in the digital age, offline interactions and traditional marketing channels still hold significant value in the real estate industry.

The Importance of Offline Networking and Marketing

Offline networking and marketing offer several advantages for women in real estate:

1. Personal Connections: Face-to-face interactions allow for building genuine relationships, establishing trust, and conveying your personality and expertise more effectively.

2. Local Presence: Offline marketing helps you connect with potential clients and referral partners in your immediate area, establishing yourself as a trusted local expert.

3. Community Engagement: Participating in local events, community organizations, and business groups demonstrates your commitment to the community and can lead to valuable connections.

4. Brand Recognition: Offline marketing materials, such as business cards, flyers, and brochures, leave a lasting impression and can increase brand awareness in your target market.

Effective Offline Networking Strategies

Here are some effective offline networking strategies for women in real estate:

1. Attend Industry Events: Participate in real estate conferences, seminars, and workshops to meet potential clients, brokers, and other professionals. Engage in conversations, exchange business cards, and follow up with valuable connections.

2. Join Professional Organizations: Actively participate in local and national real estate associations, such as the National Association of Realtors (NAR) or the National Association of Real Estate Brokers (NAREB). These organizations offer networking events, educational resources, and opportunities to connect with fellow professionals.

3. Volunteer in Your Community: Get involved in local neighborhood events, volunteer organizations, and business groups. This can help you connect with potential clients, lenders, and other key players in your community.

4. Host Open Houses and Networking Events: Organize open houses and networking events to showcase properties, meet potential buyers, and connect with other professionals in your field.

5. Leverage Referrals: Encourage existing clients, colleagues, and other professionals in your network to refer potential clients to you. Referrals can provide valuable introductions to people who may be interested in your services.

Offline Marketing Strategies for Women in Real Estate

In addition to networking, offline marketing strategies can effectively reach your target audience and establish your expertise:

1. Business Cards and Flyers: Create professional business cards and flyers that highlight your contact information, services, and unique selling proposition. Distribute them at industry events, community gatherings, and open houses.

2. Direct Mail Campaigns: Target potential clients in your area with personalized direct mail campaigns. Highlight your expertise, showcase recent success stories, and offer exclusive promotions to attract new business.

3. Door-to-door marketing: In select neighborhoods, consider door-to-door marketing to introduce yourself and your services to potential sellers or buyers. Be respectful of privacy and focus on building relationships.

4. Community Sponsorships: Sponsor local events, organizations, or charities to increase your visibility and demonstrate your commitment to the community.

5. Local Print and Online Advertising: Utilize local newspapers, magazines, and online platforms to place targeted ads. Highlight your expertise, showcase properties, and promote your services to reach a wider audience.

Integrating Offline and Online Strategies

Combining offline and online strategies creates a comprehensive marketing approach that maximizes your reach and impact:

1. Link Online Presence to Offline Materials: Include your website address, social media handles, and QR codes on your business cards, flyers, and other offline materials.

2. Promote Offline Events Online: Share information about your open houses, networking events, and community involvement on your website and social media channels.
3. Encourage Online Reviews: Direct satisfied clients to leave positive reviews on online platforms like Google My Business and Yelp. These reviews can enhance your credibility and attract new clients.
4. Track Offline Marketing Performance: Use offline marketing tracking methods, such as unique promo codes or call-tracking numbers, to measure the effectiveness of your offline campaigns.

By effectively combining offline networking and marketing strategies, women in real estate can establish a strong presence, build valuable relationships, and attract potential clients, leading to long-term success in the industry.

Chapter 5: Mastering the Art of Negotiation

5.1. The importance of negotiation in real estate

Negotiation is an essential skill for success in the real estate industry. It is the process of reaching an agreement between two or more parties, typically involving compromise and bargaining. Effective negotiation can result in favorable outcomes for both buyers and sellers, ensuring that transactions are fair, equitable, and mutually beneficial.

Negotiation plays a crucial role in various aspects of real estate transactions, including:

1. Price Negotiation: The most common negotiation in real estate involves the purchase price of a property. Buyers and sellers negotiate to reach an agreed-upon price that reflects the value of the property and the current market conditions.

2. Terms and Conditions: Negotiation extends beyond the price to encompass the terms and conditions of the sale, such as closing costs, inspection contingencies, and the timeline for completing the transaction. Both parties negotiate these terms to protect their interests and ensure a smooth process.

3. Resolving Disputes: Negotiation can be used to resolve disputes that may arise during a real estate transaction, such as disagreements over repairs, property disclosures, or any unforeseen issues. Effective negotiation can help parties reach a mutually agreeable solution without resorting to litigation.

Effective Negotiation Strategies in Real Estate

Mastering the art of negotiation in real estate requires a combination of preparation, strategy, and effective communication. Here are some key strategies to consider:

1. Do Your Research: "Do Your Research" stands as a fundamental principle for effective negotiation in the real estate industry. Thorough research provides the necessary knowledge and understanding to approach negotiations with confidence, make informed decisions, and achieve favorable outcomes.

Research plays a pivotal role in real estate negotiation by empowering both buyers and sellers to:

a. Understand Market Dynamics: By analyzing recent sales data, comparable properties, and current market trends, negotiators can gain insights into the fair market value of the property in question. This knowledge serves as a benchmark for negotiations, preventing either party from accepting an unfair price.

b. Identify Negotiation Points: Research helps identify areas where compromise might be possible. For instance, if comparable sales suggest a lower price than the asking price, the buyer has a stronger basis for negotiation. Similarly, sellers can identify potential concessions, such as covering certain closing costs, if research indicates a slower market.

c. Anticipate Counterarguments: Understanding the other party's perspective and potential counterarguments is crucial for effective negotiation. Researching the seller's recent sales history, property condition, and motivations can help anticipate their negotiating tactics and prepare accordingly.

d. Support Negotiation Strategy: Research provides the foundation for a solid negotiation strategy. By understanding the market, the property's value, and the other party's perspective, negotiators can formulate a plan that maximizes their chances of achieving their goals.

e. Build Credibility: Thorough research demonstrates professionalism and preparedness, enhancing a negotiator's credibility. When a negotiator is well-informed and can support their arguments with data, they gain the trust and respect of the other party, which can lead to more favorable outcomes.

Practical Examples of Research in Real Estate Negotiation

To illustrate the practical application of research in real estate negotiation, consider these scenarios:

a. Buyer Negotiation: A buyer interested in a property should research recent sales of similar properties in the area. This will provide insights into the fair market value and help them determine a reasonable offer price. Additionally, they should research the property's condition, reviewing inspection reports and potential renovations that may be needed.

b. Seller Negotiation: A seller should research the current market conditions, including supply and demand, interest rates, and economic factors. This will help them set a realistic asking price and anticipate potential buyer concerns. They should also research comparable sales to ensure their listing price is aligned with the market.

"Do Your Research" is a non-negotiable step in achieving successful outcomes in real estate negotiations. By gathering comprehensive information, understanding market dynamics, and anticipating counterarguments, negotiators can approach negotiations with confidence, make informed decisions, and secure favorable terms. Thorough research serves as a powerful tool for achieving win-win outcomes in the complex world of real estate transactions.

2. Set Clear Goals: Setting clear goals is a crucial step in any negotiation, and it is particularly important in the complex and dynamic world of real estate. By establishing clear objectives before entering negotiations, you can guide your actions, make informed decisions, and increase your chances of achieving a successful outcome.

Here are some key reasons why setting clear goals is essential for effective negotiation in real estate:

a. Provides Direction and Focus: Clear goals provide a roadmap for your negotiations, helping you stay focused on what you want to achieve. Without clear goals, you may be swayed by emotions or external pressures, leading to suboptimal results.

b. Defines Your Priorities: Setting clear goals helps you prioritize your objectives, ensuring that you are addressing the most important aspects of the negotiation. This prioritization allows you to allocate your energy and resources effectively.

c. Establishes Your Negotiating Range: Clear goals provide a framework for determining your negotiating range, and the acceptable range of outcomes that you are willing to consider. This range serves as a reference point for making informed compromises and concessions during the negotiation process.

d. Enhances Decision-Making: Clear goals empower you to make informed decisions during negotiations. By understanding your objectives, you can assess the implications of each proposal and make choices that align with your overall goals.

e. Facilitates Win-Win Outcomes: Setting clear goals can lead to win-win outcomes for both parties involved in the negotiation. By understanding each other's goals, you can find creative solutions that satisfy the needs of both buyers and sellers.

Here are some practical tips for setting clear goals in real estate negotiations:

a. Define Your Desired Outcome: Clearly articulate what you want to achieve in the negotiation. Whether it's maximizing your profit as a seller or securing the best possible price as a buyer, having a clear desired outcome provides direction.

b. Consider Your Alternatives: Identify your best alternative to a negotiated agreement (BATNA). This is the option you would pursue if the negotiation fails to reach a satisfactory outcome. Knowing your BATNA strengthens your negotiating position.

c. Set Realistic Expectations: Be realistic about what you can achieve in the negotiation. Consider market conditions, comparable sales, and the other party's likely objectives. Setting unrealistic expectations can lead to frustration and disappointment.

d. Prioritize Your Goals: Rank your goals in order of importance. This will help you focus on the most critical aspects of the negotiation and make informed decisions when faced with trade-offs.

e. Communicate Your Goals Clearly: Articulate your goals clearly to the other party involved in the negotiation. This transparency can foster trust and collaboration, increasing the likelihood of a mutually beneficial outcome.

By following these tips and setting clear goals, you can improve your negotiating skills, enhance your chances of success, and achieve favorable outcomes in the competitive real estate market.

3. Communicate Effectively: Communication is the cornerstone of effective negotiation, and this is especially true in the complex world of real estate transactions. Whether you are a seasoned real estate agent or a first-time homebuyer, the ability to communicate clearly, professionally, and persuasively can make all the difference in achieving your desired outcome.

The Significance of Effective Communication in Real Estate Negotiation

Effective communication plays a pivotal role in real estate negotiations for several reasons:

a. Building Rapport and Trust: Effective communication establishes rapport and trust between the negotiating parties, fostering a positive and collaborative environment. This foundation of trust is crucial for reaching mutually agreeable solutions.

b. Conveying Your Position and Understanding Others' Perspectives: Negotiation is a two-way street, and effective communication allows you to clearly articulate your goals, concerns, and priorities. It also enables you to actively listen to the other party's perspective, understanding their needs and motivations.

c. Addressing Concerns and Resolving Disputes: Clear communication is essential for addressing concerns, resolving disputes, and finding common ground. By expressing your concerns openly and respectfully, you can work with the other party to find creative solutions that address both parties' interests.

d. Managing Expectations and Avoiding Misunderstandings: Effective communication helps manage expectations and prevent misunderstandings throughout the negotiation process. By keeping the lines of communication open and addressing issues promptly, you can maintain transparency and avoid unnecessary conflicts.

Key Strategies for Effective Communication in Real Estate Negotiation

Here are some key strategies to enhance your communication skills and achieve effective negotiation outcomes:

a. Be a Good Listener: Active listening is a crucial aspect of effective communication. Make eye contact, ask clarifying questions, and avoid interrupting. Listen attentively to understand the other party's perspective, needs, and concerns.

b. Communicate Clearly and Concisely: Express your thoughts, goals, and concerns clearly and concisely. Avoid jargon or overly technical language that might confuse the other party. Use plain language that is easily understandable by all involved.

c. Be Professional and Respectful: Maintain a professional demeanor throughout the negotiation process. Address the other party with respect, even when dealing with disagreements or opposing viewpoints.

d. Be Assertive but Not Aggressive: Assertiveness is important for representing your interests effectively. However, avoid being overly aggressive or confrontational. Strike a balance between advocating for your position and maintaining a respectful tone.

e. Use Positive Language and Avoid Negatives: Frame your communication in a positive and constructive manner. Instead of focusing on negatives or blaming others, focus on finding solutions and achieving common goals.

f. Be Open to Feedback and Willing to Compromise: Negotiation often involves compromise. Be open to feedback and willing to adjust your position if necessary to reach a mutually agreeable solution.

Effective communication is a powerful tool in the real estate negotiation process. By honing your communication skills and employing these strategies, you can enhance your ability to build rapport, convey your position, address concerns, manage expectations, and ultimately achieve favorable outcomes in your real estate transactions.

4. Be Prepared to Compromise: Negotiation is a cornerstone of the real estate industry, where buyers and sellers engage in a dialogue to reach an agreement on the terms of a property transaction. Achieving a successful outcome often hinges on the ability to compromise, a crucial skill that can make or break a deal.

Compromise is the willingness to make concessions or adjustments to one's position to reach a mutually agreeable outcome. In real estate negotiations, compromise is essential because it allows both parties to achieve their desired goals to some extent.

Why Compromise is Crucial in Real Estate

- Achieving Win-Win Outcomes: Compromise enables both parties to walk away feeling satisfied, fostering a positive and lasting relationship.
- Avoiding Deadlocks and Impasses: Compromise prevents negotiations from reaching a standstill, allowing for progress and a resolution.

- Building Trust and Understanding: Compromise demonstrates a willingness to listen and consider the other party's perspective, fostering trust and understanding.
- Ensuring Smooth Transactions: Compromise promotes a smooth and efficient transaction process, minimizing delays and frustrations.

Practical Strategies for Effective Compromise

- Set Clear Goals and Priorities: Before entering negotiations, define your priorities and identify areas where you are willing to compromise.
- Listen Actively and Understand the Other Party's Perspective: Pay attention to the other party's needs and concerns, and seek to understand their motivations.
- Communicate Clearly and Professionally: Express your goals and concerns openly and respectfully, avoiding emotional language or personal attacks.
- Be Willing to Make Concessions: Approach negotiations with a flexible mindset, prepared to make some concessions to achieve a mutually beneficial outcome.
- Don't Give Up Too Easily: Negotiate from a position of strength, but don't be afraid to walk away if the deal is not favorable.

Examples of Compromise in Real Estate Negotiations

- Price Negotiation: Both parties may compromise on the price of the property, settling on a figure that reflects the fair market value and satisfies both buyer and seller.
- Closing Costs: The buyer and seller may agree to split or negotiate the allocation of closing costs, such as inspection fees and title insurance.

- Repair Negotiations: If there are repairs needed on the property, the parties may negotiate who will be responsible for the repairs and the associated costs.
- Timeline for Closing: The buyer and seller may compromise on the timeline for closing the transaction, considering their respective schedules and needs.
- Contingencies: If there are contingencies attached to the offer, such as a home inspection contingency, the parties may negotiate the terms and conditions of those contingencies.

Compromise is an essential skill for success in real estate negotiations. By approaching negotiations with a flexible mindset, a willingness to listen, and a commitment to finding common ground, both buyers and sellers can achieve favorable outcomes and build positive relationships in the dynamic world of real estate.

5. Seek Professional Guidance: Seeking professional guidance is a crucial step in enhancing your negotiation skills and achieving favorable outcomes in real estate transactions. Experienced real estate agents and attorneys can provide invaluable assistance, empowering you to navigate complex negotiations with confidence and expertise. Here are some specific benefits of seeking professional guidance:

a. Expertise and Market Knowledge: Real estate professionals possess extensive knowledge of the market, including property values, comparable sales, and current trends. They can guide you in determining a fair market value for a property, assessing the strength of your negotiating position, and understanding the nuances of specific terms and conditions.

b. Strategic Negotiation Skills: Real estate professionals are skilled negotiators who understand the psychology of bargaining and the art of compromise. They can help you develop a negotiation strategy tailored to your specific goals, anticipate counteroffers, and effectively advocate for your interests.

c. Objective Perspective: Real estate professionals can provide an objective perspective on your situation, helping you approach negotiations with clarity and rationality. They can serve as a buffer between you and the other party, managing emotions and ensuring that negotiations remain productive.

d. Legal and Regulatory Expertise: Real estate transactions involve legal and regulatory complexities that can be overwhelming for individuals without expertise. Real estate attorneys can guide you through the legal aspects of negotiations, ensuring that contracts are drafted accurately, protecting your rights, and minimizing potential risks.

e. Representation and Advocacy: Real estate professionals act as your representatives, advocating for your best interests throughout the negotiation process. They can communicate your position effectively, negotiate on your behalf, and help you reach a mutually beneficial agreement.

f. Conflict Resolution Expertise: Real estate professionals are trained to mediate and resolve disputes that may arise during negotiations. They can help parties reach a compromise, prevent disagreements from escalating, and protect the integrity of the transaction.

g. Negotiation Experience: Real estate professionals have extensive experience negotiating various types of real estate transactions, from residential purchases to complex commercial deals. They can draw upon their experience to anticipate potential challenges, identify opportunities, and guide you toward a successful outcome.

Seeking professional guidance is an investment in your success in real estate transactions. By leveraging the expertise and experience of real estate agents and attorneys, you can enhance your negotiating skills, protect your interests, and increase your chances of achieving favorable outcomes.

The Importance of Negotiation in Real Estate: A Case Study

Imagine a scenario where a buyer and seller are negotiating the purchase of a home. The seller's asking price is $300,000, but the buyer believes the fair market value is closer to $280,000. Through effective negotiation, the buyer and seller reach an agreed-upon price of $290,000. This negotiation resulted in a win-win outcome for both parties. The buyer secured the property at a price they were comfortable with, and the seller received a fair price for their home.

In conclusion, negotiation is an indispensable skill for success in the real estate industry. By mastering the art of negotiation, you can achieve favorable outcomes, protect your interests, and build strong relationships with clients and colleagues. Whether you are a buyer, seller, or real estate professional, developing strong negotiation skills will empower you to navigate the complexities of real estate transactions and achieve your goals.

5.2. How to prepare for a negotiation

Preparation is the cornerstone of successful negotiation. By thoroughly preparing for a negotiation, you can increase your chances of achieving a favorable outcome. Here's a comprehensive guide on how to prepare for a negotiation in real estate:

1. Identify Your Goals and Objectives: Clearly define your objectives for the negotiation. What do you want to achieve? Are you aiming for the highest possible price for your property as a seller, or are you seeking the best possible price for your desired home as a buyer? Having clear goals will guide your negotiation strategy and prevent you from making impulsive decisions.

2. Gather Information and Conduct Research: Equip yourself with knowledge about the property, its condition, and comparable sales in the area. Research current market trends, understand the strengths and weaknesses of the property, and identify any potential negotiation points. This information will empower you to make informed decisions during the negotiation process.

3. Evaluate Your BATNA (Best Alternative to a Negotiated Agreement): Determine your BATNA, which is the best alternative you have if negotiations fail. Consider the consequences of not reaching an agreement and identify your fallback options. Having a strong BATNA will give you leverage in the negotiation and prevent you from accepting an unfavorable outcome.

4. Understand the Other Party's Perspective: Put yourself in the other party's shoes and try to understand their motivations, goals, and concerns. This empathy will help you anticipate their actions, formulate effective counteroffers, and find common ground for a mutually agreeable solution.

5. Develop a Negotiation Plan: Outline a negotiation plan that includes your initial offer, your target price, and any contingencies or concessions you are willing to make. Having a plan will keep you focused, prevent you from giving up too easily, and help you navigate the back-and-forth of negotiation.

6. Prepare for Potential Objections: Anticipate potential objections or roadblocks that may arise during the negotiation. Practice addressing these objections confidently and persuasively, using facts, data, and logic to support your position.

7. Assemble Necessary Documentation: Gather all relevant documents, including the property appraisal, inspection reports, and any financial statements. Having this documentation readily available will demonstrate your preparedness and provide supporting evidence for your negotiation points.

8. Consider Seeking Professional Guidance: If the negotiation involves complex terms, legal aspects, or high financial stakes, consider seeking guidance from an experienced real estate agent, attorney, or mediator. Their expertise can provide valuable insights, protect your interests, and help you achieve a favorable outcome.

By following these preparation steps, you can approach your real estate negotiation with confidence, knowledge, and a clear strategy. Remember, negotiation is a dynamic process that requires flexibility, adaptability, and a willingness to compromise. By being well-prepared and understanding the art of negotiation, you can increase your chances of achieving a win-win outcome that benefits both parties.

5.3. Effective negotiation strategies

Effective negotiation can make the difference between securing a favorable deal and settling for less than you deserve. Whether you are a seasoned real estate professional or a first-time homebuyer, mastering the art of negotiation will empower you to navigate complex transactions, protect your interests, and achieve your goals.

Real estate negotiations involve a delicate balance of understanding the other party's perspective, advocating for your interests, and finding common ground to reach a mutually agreeable outcome. It is a process of communication, compromise, and strategic thinking that can significantly impact the outcome of a transaction.

Key Strategies for Effective Negotiation

1. Preparation is Key: Preparation is the cornerstone of effective negotiation. It is the process of gathering information, analyzing data, and developing a strategy to achieve your desired outcome in a negotiation. By thoroughly preparing for a negotiation, you can gain a competitive advantage, increase your chances of success, and minimize the risk of making costly mistakes.

The Significance of Preparation in Negotiation

a. Understanding the Negotiation Process: Preparation allows you to gain a deep understanding of the negotiation process, including the different stages, potential issues, and common negotiation tactics. This knowledge empowers you to anticipate the other party's moves and react effectively.

b. Identifying Your Goals and Interests: Clearly defined goals and interests provide a roadmap for your negotiation. They help you stay focused on what you want to achieve and avoid being swayed by distractions or pressure tactics.

c. Conducting Thorough Research: Researching the property, market conditions, and comparable sales provides you with valuable information to support your negotiating position. This knowledge can help you determine a fair price, identify potential leverage points, and make informed decisions.

d. Assessing the Other Party's Perspective: Understanding the other party's goals, interests, and concerns can help you develop a negotiation strategy that addresses their needs and creates a win-win situation.

e. Anticipating Potential Issues: By anticipating potential issues that may arise during the negotiation, you can prepare responses and contingency plans. This proactive approach can prevent setbacks and maintain momentum toward your desired outcome.

Preparation is not just about gathering information; it's about developing a strategic mindset and a clear understanding of your negotiating objectives. By investing time and effort into preparation, you can enhance your negotiation skills, increase your confidence, and achieve more favorable outcomes in your real estate transactions.

2. Establish Rapport and Build Trust: Establishing rapport and building trust are crucial components of effective negotiation. These foundational elements set the stage for a collaborative and productive negotiation process, increasing the likelihood of achieving mutually beneficial outcomes for all parties involved.

Rapport is a connection or relationship characterized by mutual understanding, trust, and respect. It is the feeling of being "in sync" with another person, where communication flows naturally and both parties feel comfortable expressing their thoughts and ideas.

Rapport plays a pivotal role in negotiation for several reasons:

a. Reduces Tension and Creates a Positive Environment: A rapport-based environment fosters a sense of ease and comfort, lowering tensions and allowing for more open and constructive discussions.

b. Encourages Empathy and Understanding: Rapport enables negotiators to better understand each other's perspectives, motivations, and concerns. This empathy leads to more informed decision-making and a greater willingness to compromise.

c. Increases Trust and Credibility: Trust is essential for successful negotiation, as it allows parties to feel secure in sharing information and making agreements. Rapport fosters trust, making negotiators more receptive to each other's proposals.

d. Promotes Collaboration and Problem-Solving: A rapport-based relationship encourages collaboration and joint problem-solving. Negotiators are more likely to work together to find creative solutions when they trust and respect each other.

Strategies for Establishing Rapport and Building Trust in Negotiation

- Active Listening: Actively listen to the other party's comments, demonstrating genuine interest in their perspective. This shows respect and encourages them to open up more fully.
- Positive Nonverbal Cues: Maintain eye contact, smile, and use open body language to convey warmth and approachability. Nonverbal cues can significantly impact the negotiation atmosphere.

- Empathy and Understanding: Acknowledge the other party's feelings and concerns, even if you disagree with them. Showing empathy fosters a sense of connection and trust.
- Common Ground: Identify areas of shared interests or values. Finding common ground creates a foundation for further connection and collaboration.
- Transparency and Honesty: Be transparent about your intentions and avoid making misleading statements. Honesty builds trust and credibility.
- Appreciation and Acknowledgement: Recognize and appreciate the other party's contributions and insights. This shows respect and encourages continued engagement.

Building rapport and trust takes time and effort, and it requires consistent demonstration of these qualities throughout the negotiation process. By prioritizing rapport and trust, negotiators can create a more positive and productive environment, increasing the likelihood of reaching mutually beneficial outcomes.

3. Effectively Communicate Your Position: Effectively communicating your position is a cornerstone of successful negotiation. It allows you to clearly convey your goals, interests, and needs to the other party, fostering understanding and laying the foundation for a mutually beneficial agreement.

Effective communication in negotiation serves several crucial purposes:

- Clarity of Intent: It ensures that your goals and expectations are clearly understood by the other party, preventing misunderstandings and misinterpretations.
- Building Trust and Rapport: Clear and respectful communication fosters trust and rapport, creating a more conducive environment for reaching an agreement.
- Demonstrating Expertise: Articulating your position effectively showcases your knowledge and expertise, establishing credibility and strengthening your bargaining power.
- Active Listening and Understanding: Effective communication involve not just speaking but also actively listening to the other party's perspective, allowing for a more comprehensive understanding of their needs and concerns.
- Finding Common Ground: By communicating effectively, you can identify areas of common ground and potential compromise, facilitating the development of a mutually acceptable solution.

Effective Communication Strategies for Negotiation

- Clarity and Conciseness: Convey your message clearly and concisely, avoiding jargon or overly complex language. Use simple, direct language that is easy for the other party to understand.
- Active Listening: Practice active listening, giving the other party your full attention and demonstrating that you value their perspective. Ask clarifying questions to ensure you understand their position.
- Empathy and Respect: Acknowledge the other party's position and concerns, even if you disagree. Show

empathy and respect, creating a more collaborative atmosphere.

- Focus on Interests, Not Positions: Separate underlying interests from stated positions. Focus on finding solutions that address both parties' core interests rather than simply defending entrenched positions.
- Nonverbal Cues: Be mindful of your nonverbal communication. Maintain eye contact, use a calm and professional demeanor, and avoid fidgeting or interrupting.

Effectively Communicating Your Position: A Practical Example

Imagine you are negotiating the purchase of a home. The seller's asking price is $350,000, but you believe the fair market value is closer to $320,000. Instead of simply stating your desired price, you could effectively communicate your position by:

- Explaining Your Valuation: Provide evidence to support your valuation, such as recent comparable sales in the area. Explain your reasoning and demonstrate your knowledge of the market.
- Acknowledging the Seller's Perspective: Acknowledge the seller's asking price and their attachment to the property. Show empathy and understanding for their position.
- Proposing a Compromise: Propose a compromise price that reflects your valuation while also considering the seller's expectations. Be open to further negotiation and finding a middle ground.

- Highlight Benefits: Emphasize the benefits of working with you, such as a quick and hassle-free closing or your willingness to handle certain aspects of the transaction.
- Maintain a Professional Tone: Throughout the negotiation, maintain a professional and respectful tone. Avoid making personal attacks or using accusatory language.

By effectively communicating your position, you can navigate negotiations with greater confidence, increase your chances of reaching a favorable outcome, and establish a positive reputation as a skilled negotiator.

4. Be a Good Listener: Effective listening is a critical skill for success in any field, and it is particularly important in the dynamic and complex world of real estate negotiations. By actively listening to the other party, you can gain valuable insights into their needs, perspectives, and motivations, which can help you formulate a more effective negotiating strategy.

Active listening goes beyond simply hearing the words being spoken; it involves paying close attention to both verbal and nonverbal cues, demonstrating empathy, and striving to understand the underlying meaning of the other party's communication. By actively listening, you can reap several benefits in real estate negotiations:

a. Build Rapport and Trust: Active listening shows respect and consideration for the other party, fostering rapport and trust, which are essential for building a collaborative negotiating environment.

b. Understand Their Perspective: Active listening allows you to gain a deeper understanding of the other party's needs, priorities, and concerns. This knowledge can help you tailor your approach and address their specific motivations.

c. Identify Opportunities: Active listening can reveal opportunities to create value for the other party, leading to more mutually beneficial outcomes.

d. Anticipate Counterarguments and Concerns: Understanding the other party's perspective allows you to anticipate their counterarguments and concerns, enabling you to prepare effective responses.

e. Detect Underlying Emotions and Intentions: Active listening can reveal the underlying emotions and intentions of the other party, providing clues to their true negotiating style and priorities.

Strategies for Effective Listening in Real Estate Negotiations

To actively listen effectively in real estate negotiations, consider the following strategies:

- Eliminate Distractions: Minimize distractions such as phones, laptops, or background noise to fully focus on the other party's communication.
- Maintain Eye Contact: Eye contact demonstrates attentiveness and conveys respect for the other party's words.
- Use Encouraging Body Language: Nod your head, maintain an open posture, and use positive facial expressions to show engagement and understanding.
- Paraphrase and Ask Clarifying Questions: Repeating key points and asking clarifying questions demonstrate that

you are listening carefully and seeking to fully understand their perspective.

- Avoid Interrupting or Reacting Defensively: Allow the other party to express their thoughts and feelings without interruption. Respond with empathy and understanding, even if you disagree with their viewpoint.
- Summarize Key Points: Regularly summarize the main points of the discussion to ensure you have a clear understanding of their position.

Effective listening is not about simply waiting for your turn to speak; it's about actively engaging with the other party to gain a deeper understanding of their perspective. By incorporating active listening into your negotiation strategies, you can build stronger relationships, identify mutually beneficial solutions, and achieve your goals in the competitive world of real estate negotiations.

5. Embrace Compromise and Flexibility: Compromise and flexibility are two essential qualities for effective negotiation, particularly in the real estate industry, where deals often involve significant financial considerations and complex terms and conditions. By embracing compromise and flexibility, negotiators can increase their chances of achieving mutually beneficial outcomes and building strong relationships with their counterparts.

Compromise is the act of finding a middle ground between two opposing positions. It involves acknowledging the other party's perspective and making concessions to reach a common understanding. In real estate negotiations, compromise is often crucial for closing deals and avoiding costly legal disputes.

Benefits of Embracing Compromise

a. Achieving Win-Win Outcomes: Compromise allows both parties to walk away from the negotiation feeling satisfied, rather than having one party feel like they have lost.

b. Preserving Relationships: Compromise can help maintain positive relationships between buyers, sellers, and real estate agents, fostering future collaboration and opportunities.

c. Avoiding Escalation: By being willing to compromise, parties can prevent negotiations from reaching a deadlock or escalating into conflict.

Flexibility is the ability to adapt to changing circumstances and adjust one's approach as needed. In real estate negotiations, flexibility allows negotiators to respond to unexpected challenges and find creative solutions to overcome obstacles.

Benefits of Embracing Flexibility

a. Navigating Complexities: Real estate transactions often involve intricate details and unforeseen issues. Flexibility allows negotiators to adapt to these complexities and find solutions that work for all parties.

b. Seizing Opportunities: Flexibility can enable negotiators to identify and capitalize on new opportunities that arise during the negotiation process.

c. Building Trust: When negotiators demonstrate flexibility, it builds trust and confidence with their counterparts, leading to more collaborative and productive negotiations.

Strategies for Embracing Compromise and Flexibility

a. Empathy and Understanding: Cultivate empathy for the other party's perspective and try to understand their needs and concerns. This can lead to more meaningful compromises and solutions.

b. Focus on Common Goals: Identify shared goals that both parties value and work towards achieving those goals collaboratively. This can help align priorities and promote mutually beneficial outcomes.

c. Creative Thinking: Approach negotiations with an open mind and be willing to explore creative solutions that may not have been considered initially.

d. Communication and Collaboration: Maintain open communication throughout the negotiation process, actively listen to the other party's feedback, and work together to find common ground.

Compromise and flexibility are not signs of weakness; they are hallmarks of effective negotiation. By embracing these qualities, negotiators can navigate the complexities of real estate transactions, achieve favorable outcomes, and build strong relationships that benefit everyone involved.

6. Consider Creative Solutions: In any negotiation, seeking creative solutions is a crucial strategy for achieving mutually beneficial outcomes. This approach involves moving beyond conventional thinking and exploring unconventional options to find solutions that address the underlying interests of all parties involved.

Traditional negotiation often focuses on bargaining over price or terms, but creative solutions can expand the possibilities and lead to more satisfactory outcomes. By considering creative approaches, negotiators can:

a. Address Underlying Interests: Creative solutions focus on understanding the underlying interests and motivations of each party, rather than simply focusing on fixed positions. This deeper understanding can lead to solutions that address the core needs of all parties involved.

b. Expand the Pie: Creative solutions can expand the pie of value by uncovering new opportunities or identifying areas where both parties can benefit. This approach can lead to win-win outcomes that are not possible through traditional negotiation.

c. Build Relationships: Seeking creative solutions can foster a more collaborative and supportive negotiation environment. This can lead to stronger relationships and increased trust between the parties, which can benefit future interactions.

Finding creative solutions requires a willingness to think outside the box and explore unconventional options. Here are some strategies to consider:

- Brainstorming: Gather the parties involved and encourage open-minded brainstorming to generate a wide range of ideas, no matter how unconventional they may seem.
- Seek Input from Others: Consult with neutral third parties, such as experienced mediators or facilitators, who can provide fresh perspectives and help identify creative solutions.
- Visualize Alternative Scenarios: Imagine different scenarios and potential outcomes to break free from fixed patterns of thinking and explore new possibilities.
- Consider Multiple Perspectives: Approach the negotiation from different angles, considering the needs

and perspectives of all parties involved. This can lead to solutions that address the specific concerns of each party.

- Embrace Experimentation: Be open to trying new approaches and experimenting with different ideas. This willingness to experiment can lead to unexpected breakthroughs and innovative solutions.

Examples of Creative Solutions in Real Estate Negotiation

Creative solutions can be applied to various aspects of real estate negotiations. Here are a few examples:

a. Seller Financing: In cases where a buyer may struggle to secure traditional financing, a seller may offer creative financing options, such as owner-carryback financing or seller financing, to facilitate the sale.

b. Lease-to-Own Arrangements: For buyers who may not be ready to purchase immediately, a lease-to-own arrangement can provide a pathway to ownership while allowing them to test the property and accumulate funds for a future purchase.

c. Contingent Offers: Creative contingencies can address specific concerns or needs of either party, such as allowing a buyer to sell their current home before closing on the new property or providing a longer closing timeline for a seller who needs more time to relocate.

d. Shared Equity Structures: In some situations, a creative solution may involve a shared equity structure, where both the buyer and seller share ownership of the property, potentially reducing the upfront purchase price for the buyer.

e. Community Benefits: In cases involving properties with community impact, creative solutions may include dedicating a portion of the property for community use, providing affordable housing options, or establishing partnerships with local organizations to benefit the neighborhood.

In conclusion, in the dynamic world of real estate, embracing creative solutions can lead to more favorable outcomes and mutually beneficial agreements. By moving beyond traditional negotiation approaches and exploring unconventional options, parties can address underlying interests, expand the pie of value, and build stronger relationships. As a key strategy for effective negotiation, seeking creative solutions empowers negotiators to navigate complex transactions and achieve successful results.

7. Leverage Silence and Walk-Away Power:

Leverage Silence and Walk-Away Power are two crucial strategies for effective negotiation. They are powerful tools that can be used to influence the outcome of negotiations and achieve favorable results.

Leveraging Silence

Silence is often underestimated in negotiations. It can be a powerful tool to create anticipation, gather information, and control the pace of negotiations. By using silence strategically, you can:

- Give the other party time to think and respond: Silence can give the other party time to process your offer or argument and formulate their response. This can lead to more thoughtful and considered responses.
- Put pressure on the other party: Silence can also put pressure on the other party to respond. They may feel

uncomfortable with the silence and be more willing to make concessions to fill the void.

- Demonstrate confidence and control: Using silence effectively can convey confidence and control, signaling to the other party that you are in no rush to settle and are willing to walk away if necessary.

Walk-Away Power

Walk-away power is the ability and willingness to walk away from a negotiation if it is not in your best interests. This power is essential for effective negotiation, as it demonstrates to the other party that you have alternatives and are not dependent on the deal. By having walk-away power, you can:

- Avoid settling for less than you deserve: If the other party is not willing to meet your reasonable demands, being prepared to walk away can prevent you from settling for less than you deserve.
- Increase your bargaining leverage: Having walk away power can increase your bargaining leverage. The other party will be more likely to negotiate in good faith if they know you are willing to walk away.
- Maintain control over the negotiation: Walking away from a negotiation demonstrates that you are in control and are not willing to be taken advantage of.

Combining Silence and Walk-Away Power

The most effective use of these two strategies often involves combining them. By using silence strategically and demonstrating that you have walk-away power, you can put significant pressure on the other party to make concessions and reach a mutually agreeable outcome.

Examples of Using Silence and Walk-Away Power in Real Estate Negotiations

Here are a few examples of how silence and walk-away power can be used effectively in real estate negotiations:

- A seller sets a high asking price for their home and remains silent when the buyer makes an initial offer. The seller's silence forces the buyer to consider their offer and may encourage them to increase it.
- A buyer makes a low initial offer on a property and then remains silent when the seller responds with a counteroffer. The buyer's silence communicates that they are serious about their offer and may encourage the seller to lower their price.
- An experienced real estate agent representing a buyer walks away from a negotiation when the seller is unwilling to make reasonable concessions. The agent's walk-away power demonstrates that they are serious about their client's interests and are not afraid to walk away if necessary.

In conclusion, leveraging silence and walk-away power are two crucial strategies for effective negotiation. By using these tools strategically, you can increase your bargaining leverage, achieve more favorable outcomes, and protect your interests in real estate transactions.

8. Seek Professional Guidance:

Seeking professional guidance is a crucial strategy for effective negotiation, especially in complex real estate transactions. Real estate transactions involve significant financial investments, intricate legal considerations, and a multitude of factors that can influence the outcome of negotiations. Engaging a knowledgeable and experienced professional can provide invaluable support and expertise, enhancing your negotiating position and increasing your chances of securing a favorable outcome.

Benefits of Seeking Professional Guidance

a. Expert Knowledge and Insights: Real estate professionals possess in-depth knowledge of the market, property values, and negotiation tactics. They can provide valuable insights into comparable sales, current trends, and strategies for maximizing your bargaining power.

b. Objective Perspective and Advocacy: Real estate professionals act as impartial advisors, providing an objective perspective on the negotiation process. They can advocate for your interests, protect your rights, and ensure that your goals are considered throughout the process.

c. Navigational Expertise: Real estate transactions involve a myriad of legal and technical aspects, such as contract terms, disclosures, and due diligence procedures. Experienced professionals can guide you through these complexities, ensuring that your transaction complies with legal requirements and protects your interests.

d. Emotion Management: Negotiations can be emotionally charged, especially when dealing with significant financial investments. Real estate professionals can help you manage your emotions, maintain a calm and professional demeanor, and avoid making impulsive decisions.

e. Networking and Connections: Real estate professionals have established networks of contacts, including lenders, appraisers, inspectors, and other relevant parties. These connections can facilitate the negotiation process, provide access to valuable information, and streamline the transaction.

When to Seek Professional Guidance

a. Complex Transactions: Involving high-value properties, multiple parties, or intricate legal issues, complex transactions warrant professional guidance to navigate the complexities and protect your interests.

b. Lack of Experience: If you are a first-time buyer or seller, or lack experience in real estate negotiations, seeking professional guidance can provide you with the knowledge and expertise to make informed decisions.

c. Language or Cultural Barriers: If language or cultural barriers pose challenges in communicating effectively, professional assistance can ensure clear understanding and prevent misinterpretations.

d. Time Constraints: If you have limited time to dedicate to negotiations, seeking professional guidance can alleviate the burden and ensure that your interests are represented effectively.

Choosing the Right Professional

- Experience and Reputation: Choose a real estate professional with a proven track record of success in negotiating favorable outcomes for their clients. Seek recommendations from trusted sources and research their credentials and experience.
- Communication and Trust: Establish open and transparent communication with your chosen professional. Discuss your goals, concerns, and

expectations clearly to ensure a strong working relationship built on trust and mutual understanding.

- Specialization: Consider the specific type of property or transaction involved and seek a professional with expertise in that area. This ensures that you receive tailored advice and strategies aligned with your specific needs.

Seeking professional guidance is a strategic investment that can significantly enhance your negotiating position in real estate transactions. By engaging an experienced and knowledgeable real estate professional, you can gain valuable insights, protect your interests, and increase your chances of achieving a favorable outcome that meets your goals and objectives.

A Case Study: Effective Negotiation in Action

A buyer is interested in purchasing a property listed for $350,000. Through thorough research, they determined that the fair market value is closer to $320,000. The buyer approaches the seller with an initial offer of $320,000, explaining their rationale and providing supporting evidence.

The seller is initially resistant, but through open communication and a willingness to compromise, the parties reach an agreed-upon price of $330,000. The buyer secures the property at a favorable price, and the seller achieves a fair return on their investment. This outcome demonstrates the effectiveness of negotiation in reaching mutually beneficial results.

To conclude, Effective negotiation is a valuable skill that can make a significant impact on your success in real estate. By mastering the art of communication, understanding the other party's perspective, and employing strategic tactics, you can navigate complex transactions and achieve your goals. Whether you are buying, selling, or investing in real estate, developing strong negotiation skills will empower you to make informed decisions and secure favorable outcomes.

Chapter 6: Financing Your Real Estate Goals

6.1. Understanding the different types of real estate loans

Purchasing real estate is a significant financial decision, and securing the right financing is crucial to achieving your goals. Real estate loans provide the necessary funds to purchase a property, and there are various types of loans available with different terms, interest rates, and eligibility requirements. Understanding the different types of real estate loans is essential for making an informed decision that aligns with your financial situation and long-term objectives.

Types of Real Estate Loans

1. Conventional Loans: Conventional loans are the most common type of real estate financing, offered by banks, credit unions, and other financial institutions. They are not backed by the government, unlike FHA, VA, and USDA loans. Conventional loans typically require a down payment of 20% of the purchase price and a good credit score.

Advantages of Conventional Loans

Conventional loans offer several advantages over other types of real estate loans:

a. Lower interest rates: Conventional loans typically have lower interest rates than government-backed loans. This is because conventional loans are not insured by the government, which reduces the lender's risk.

b. More flexibility: Conventional loans offer more flexibility in terms of down payment amounts and credit score requirements. Some lenders may allow down payments as low as 3% for well-qualified borrowers.

c. No private mortgage insurance (PMI): Once the loan-to-value (LTV) ratio reaches 80%, borrowers with conventional loans no longer have to pay PMI. PMI is an additional monthly fee that protects the lender in case the borrower defaults on the loan.

d. Faster approval process: Conventional loans typically have a faster approval process than government-backed loans. This is because conventional lenders do not have to follow the same strict underwriting guidelines as government-backed lenders.

Disadvantages of Conventional Loans

Conventional loans also have some disadvantages:

a. Higher credit score requirements: Conventional loans typically require a good credit score of 620 or higher. This can make it difficult for borrowers with poor credit to qualify for a conventional loan.

b. Larger down payment: Conventional loans typically require a down payment of 20% of the purchase price. This can make it difficult for borrowers to save up enough money to buy a home.

Eligibility for Conventional Loans

To be eligible for a conventional loan, you must meet the following criteria:

- Good credit score: A credit score of 620 or higher is typically required.
- Debt-to-income ratio (DTI): Your DTI, which is the percentage of your monthly income that goes towards debt payments, should be 43% or lower.

- Steady employment: You must have a steady job for at least two years.
- Sufficient savings: You must have enough savings to cover the down payment and closing costs.

Tips for Getting a Conventional Loan

If you are considering getting a conventional loan, there are a few things you can do to improve your chances of approval:

- Check your credit score: Get a copy of your credit report and check your score. Make sure there are no errors on your report and work to improve your score if it is below 620.
- Pay down debt: Reduce your debt-to-income ratio by paying down your outstanding debts. This will make you a more attractive borrower to lenders.
- Save up for a down payment: Aim to save up at least 20% of the purchase price of the home you want to buy. This will reduce the amount you need to borrow and make your loan more affordable.
- Get pre-approved for a mortgage: Getting pre-approved for a mortgage will show sellers that you are a serious buyer and make your offer more attractive.
- Shop around for the best interest rate: Compare interest rates from different lenders to find the best deal.

Conventional loans are a good option for borrowers with good credit and a steady income who can afford a 20% down payment. If you meet the eligibility criteria, a conventional loan can provide you with a lower interest rate and more flexibility than a government-backed loan.

2. Government-Backed Loans: Government-backed loans, also known as federally insured loans, are a type of real estate financing that is insured by the federal government. This insurance protects lenders, allowing them to offer lower interest rates and more favorable terms to borrowers with lower credit scores or smaller down payments. Government-backed loans play a significant role in the real estate market, making homeownership more accessible to a wider range of individuals and families.

Types of Government-Backed Loans

There are three main types of government-backed loans:

- FHA Loans: FHA loans are insured by the Federal Housing Administration (FHA). They are known for their lower minimum credit score requirements, typically starting at 580, and down payment options as low as 3.5%. FHA loans are particularly beneficial for first-time homebuyers or those with less credit history.
- VA Loans: VA loans are guaranteed by the Department of Veterans Affairs (VA). They are specifically designed for eligible veterans, active-duty military personnel, and surviving spouses. VA loans offer no down payment requirement and competitive interest rates, making them an attractive option for veterans seeking homeownership.
- USDA Loans: USDA loans are insured by the United States Department of Agriculture (USDA). They are primarily intended for borrowers in rural and suburban areas with limited access to conventional financing. USDA loans offer lower credit score requirements, typically starting at 580, and no down payment for eligible borrowers.

Benefits of Government-Backed Loans

Government-backed loans offer several advantages over conventional loans, including:

a. Lower Credit Score Requirements: Government-backed loans generally have lower minimum credit score requirements than conventional loans. This makes them more accessible to borrowers with less credit history or past credit issues.

b. Smaller Down Payments: Government-backed loans often allow for smaller down payments, sometimes as low as 3.5% or even 0% for eligible borrowers. This can significantly reduce the upfront financial burden of purchasing a home.

c. Lower Interest Rates: Government-backed loans typically offer lower interest rates compared to conventional loans, resulting in lower monthly payments and overall loan costs.

d. Government Guarantee: The government guarantee provides protection to lenders, reducing their risk and allowing them to offer more favorable loan terms to borrowers.

Eligibility for Government-Backed Loans

Eligibility for government-backed loans varies depending on the specific program and the borrower's circumstances. However, some general eligibility requirements include:

- Credit Score: Borrowers must meet the minimum credit score requirements for the specific loan program.
- Income Requirements: Borrowers must demonstrate sufficient income to afford the mortgage payments and maintain a stable financial situation.
- Property Eligibility: The property being financed must meet certain requirements, such as being located in an

eligible area and adhering to property condition standards.

- Veteran Status: For VA loans, borrowers must be eligible veterans, active-duty military personnel, or surviving spouses.
- Rural or Suburban Residence: For USDA loans, borrowers must be purchasing a home in a designated rural or suburban area.

Applying for Government-Backed Loans

The process of applying for government-backed loans typically involves the following steps:

- Pre-Approval: Obtaining pre-approval from a lender allows you to determine your loan eligibility and maximum borrowing capacity.
- Finding a Property: Once pre-approved, you can begin searching for a property that meets your needs and eligibility criteria.
- Submitting an Offer: Once you find a suitable property, you can submit an offer to purchase it, contingent upon mortgage approval.
- Formal Loan Application: The formal loan application process involves providing documentation of your income, assets, and credit history.
- Underwriting and Approval: The lender will underwrite your loan application to assess your creditworthiness and ability to repay the loan.
- Closing Process: Upon loan approval, the closing process involves finalizing the loan documents, paying closing costs, and transferring ownership of the property.

Government-backed loans play a vital role in expanding homeownership opportunities and promoting financial stability for individuals and families. By offering lower credit score requirements, smaller down payments, and competitive interest rates, these loans make homeownership more attainable for a wider range of borrowers. If you are considering purchasing a home, exploring government-backed loans can provide valuable options and potential advantages in your real estate journey.

3. Adjustable-Rate Mortgages (ARMs): Adjustable-Rate Mortgages (ARMs), also known as variable-rate or floating mortgages, are a type of real estate loan that offers an initial low-interest rate that adjusts periodically based on market conditions. ARMs are typically offered with fixed-rate introductory periods, ranging from 3 to 10 years, during which the interest rate remains constant. After the introductory period ends, the interest rate adjusts regularly, usually at monthly or annual intervals.

Benefits of Adjustable-Rate Mortgages (ARMs)

a. Lower Initial Interest Rates: ARMs typically offer lower initial interest rates compared to fixed-rate mortgages, resulting in lower monthly payments during the introductory period. This can be particularly attractive for borrowers seeking to maximize cash flow in the early years of homeownership.

b. Flexibility: ARMs provide flexibility in adjusting to changing market conditions. If interest rates decline, the adjustable rate will also decrease, potentially lowering your monthly payments.

c. Potential for Savings: If interest rates remain low or decline during the initial fixed-rate period, borrowers may enjoy significant savings over fixed-rate mortgages.

Risks of Adjustable-Rate Mortgages (ARMs)

a. Interest Rate Fluctuations: The primary risk associated with ARMs is the potential for interest rate fluctuations. If interest rates rise, the adjustable rate will also increase, leading to higher monthly payments. This can strain household budgets and make it difficult to manage finances.

b. Unpredictable Payments: The unpredictability of future payments can be a major concern for borrowers with fixed incomes or those seeking stability in their monthly expenses.

c. Potential for Negative Amortization: In scenarios where interest rates exceed the principal payments, negative amortization can occur, causing the loan balance to grow instead of decline. This can prolong the repayment period and increase the overall cost of the loan.

Suitability of Adjustable-Rate Mortgages (ARMs)

ARMs may be suitable for borrowers who:

- Have a short-term horizon for homeownership and plan to sell or refinance before the introductory period ends.
- Have a strong financial position and are comfortable with the risk of interest rate fluctuations.
- Anticipate declining interest rates shortly.
- Prioritize lower initial monthly payments and are willing to accept the potential for higher payments later.

Considerations for Borrowers Choosing ARMs

Before opting for an ARM, borrowers should carefully consider the following factors:

- Financial Stability: Assess your financial situation and ability to handle potential increases in monthly payments if interest rates rise.
- Risk Tolerance: Evaluate your risk tolerance and comfort level with the unpredictability of adjustable interest rates.
- Time Horizon: Consider your long-term plans for the property and whether you intend to stay in it for an extended period.
- Comparison with Fixed-Rate Mortgages: Compare the long-term costs and interest rates of ARMs with fixed-rate mortgages to determine which option aligns better with your financial goals.
- Expert Guidance: Seek advice from a mortgage specialist or financial advisor to understand the terms, risks, and suitability of ARMs in your specific circumstances.

Adjustable-Rate Mortgages (ARMs) can be an attractive option for borrowers seeking lower initial interest rates and flexibility in adjusting to market conditions. However, it is crucial to carefully consider the potential risks of interest rate fluctuations and the impact on your financial stability before committing to an ARM. Consulting with a mortgage specialist or financial advisor can provide valuable insights and help you make an informed decision that aligns with your long-term financial goals and risk tolerance.

4. Fixed-Rate Mortgages (FRMs): Fixed-rate mortgages (FRMs) are among the most popular types of real estate loans, offering borrowers stability and predictability in their monthly mortgage payments. Unlike adjustable-rate mortgages (ARMs), which have interest rates that fluctuate periodically based on market conditions, FRMs provide a constant interest rate throughout the loan term. This stability is particularly appealing to borrowers who prefer consistent payments and want to protect against interest rate fluctuations.

Characteristics of Fixed-Rate Mortgages

FRMs are characterized by several key features:

- Constant Interest Rate: The interest rate on an FRM remains fixed throughout the loan term, typically ranging from 15 to 30 years. This stability allows borrowers to budget effectively and plan for future expenses.
- Predictable Monthly Payments: With a fixed interest rate, monthly mortgage payments remain consistent throughout the loan term. This predictability helps borrowers manage their finances and avoid surprises.
- Protection Against Interest Rate Fluctuations: FRMs shield borrowers from the risk of rising interest rates, which can significantly impact monthly payments. This protection is particularly valuable during periods of economic uncertainty.

Suitability of Fixed-Rate Mortgages

FRMs are well-suited for borrowers who:

- Prefer Predictable Payments: Borrowers who prioritize consistent monthly payments and financial stability often find FRMs to be the ideal choice.
- Seek Protection Against Interest Rate Fluctuations: Borrowers who are concerned about rising interest

rates and their impact on monthly payments often prefer the stability of FRMs.

- Plan to Stay in the Property Long-Term: Borrowers who intend to remain in the property they finance for an extended period can benefit from the consistent payments and interest rate protection offered by FRMs.

Benefits of Fixed-Rate Mortgages

FRMs offer several advantages for borrowers:

- Predictable Budgeting: Fixed interest rates allow borrowers to accurately budget for their monthly mortgage payments and plan for future expenses.
- Protection Against Rising Interest Rates: FRMs safeguard borrowers from the financial burden of rising interest rates, ensuring stable monthly payments throughout the loan term.
- Peace of Mind: The stability and predictability of FRMs provide borrowers with peace of mind, allowing them to focus on other aspects of homeownership.

Considerations for Fixed-Rate Mortgages

While FRMs offer distinct advantages, there are a few considerations to keep in mind:

- Initial Interest Rates: FRMs typically have higher initial interest rates compared to ARMs. However, the stability of fixed payments over the loan term can offset this initial difference.
- Early Prepayment Penalties: Some FRMs may have prepayment penalties if the loan is paid off early.

Borrowers should carefully review the terms of their mortgage to understand any associated penalties.

- Refinancing Options: If market conditions change and interest rates decline, borrowers may consider refinancing their FRM to a lower interest rate. However, refinancing costs and eligibility should be evaluated before proceeding.

Fixed-rate mortgages (FRMs) remain a popular choice among real estate borrowers due to the stability and predictability they offer. By providing consistent monthly payments and protection against interest rate fluctuations, FRMs allow borrowers to make sound financial decisions and plan for their future with greater certainty. Whether you are a first-time homebuyer or an experienced investor, understanding the features and benefits of FRMs can empower you to make informed choices and achieve your real estate goals.

5. Jumbo Loans: Jumbo loans, also known as jumbo mortgages, are a type of mortgage financing that exceeds the conforming loan limits set by Fannie Mae and Freddie Mac, government-sponsored enterprises that purchase and securitize mortgages. These loans are considered non-conforming loans because they do not adhere to the guidelines established by these agencies. Jumbo loans are typically used to finance properties that are more expensive than those that can be financed with conventional mortgages.

Key Characteristics of Jumbo Loans

a. Higher Loan Amounts: Jumbo loans typically start at $726,200, the conforming loan limit for a single-family home in most counties in the United States (except Hawaii and Alaska and a few federally designated high-cost markets, where the limit is $1,089,300).

b. Stricter Qualification Requirements: Due to the higher loan amounts and perceived greater risk, jumbo loans have stricter qualification requirements compared to conventional mortgages. Borrowers typically need higher credit scores, lower debt-to-income (DTI) ratios, and larger down payments to qualify for jumbo loans.

c. Varying Interest Rates: Interest rates for jumbo loans can vary depending on the lender, market conditions, and the borrower's creditworthiness. While jumbo loan interest rates may be slightly higher than conventional loan rates, they have generally trended closer to conventional rates in recent years.

Types of Jumbo Loans

Jumbo loans are available for a variety of property types, including:

- Single-family homes: The most common type of property financed with jumbo loans.
- Condominiums: Jumbo loans can be used to purchase condominiums in high-cost markets.
- Investment properties: Jumbo loans can be used to finance investment properties, such as rental properties or vacation homes.

Benefits of Jumbo Loans

Jumbo loans offer several benefits to borrowers, including:

- Access to More Expensive Properties: Jumbo loans allow borrowers to finance properties that exceed conventional loan limits, providing access to a wider range of housing options.
- Flexibility in Property Choice: Borrowers can choose from a variety of property types, including luxury

homes, large homes in high-cost areas, and unique properties that may not fall under conventional loan guidelines.

- Potential for Higher Appreciation: Properties financed with jumbo loans may have higher appreciation potential due to their location, features, or desirability.

Considerations for Jumbo Loans

Before taking out a jumbo loan, it is important to consider the following:

- Stricter Qualification Requirements: Jumbo loans require higher credit scores, lower debt-to-income ratios, and larger down payments compared to conventional loans. Ensure you meet these requirements before applying.
- Higher Interest Rates: While jumbo loan interest rates have trended closer to conventional rates, they may still be slightly higher. Be prepared for slightly higher monthly payments.
- Limited Lender Options: Not all lenders offer jumbo loans, and those that do may have more stringent application processes. Shop around and compare different lenders to find the best terms.

Obtaining a Jumbo Loan

To obtain a jumbo loan, follow these steps:

- Check Your Credit Score: Review your credit score and make sure it meets the lender's requirements.

- Gather Financial Documentation: Prepare financial documents, such as tax returns, pay stubs, and bank statements, to demonstrate your financial stability.
- Shop Around for Lenders: Compare interest rates, terms, and fees from different lenders to find the most favorable loan option.
- Obtain Pre-Approval: Get pre-approved for a jumbo loan to demonstrate your financial capacity to potential sellers.
- Work with an Experienced Real Estate Agent: Partner with an experienced real estate agent who is familiar with jumbo loans and can guide you through the process.

Jumbo loans offer a valuable financing option for borrowers seeking to purchase properties that exceed conventional loan limits. By understanding the characteristics, benefits, and considerations of jumbo loans, borrowers can make informed decisions and navigate the process effectively to secure the financing they need to achieve their real estate goals.

Choosing the Right Real Estate Loan

Selecting the appropriate real estate loan depends on various factors, including:

1. Credit Score: Your credit score plays a significant role in determining the loan options and interest rates available to you. A higher credit score indicates lower risk and translates into better loan terms.

2. Down Payment: The amount of down payment you can afford will influence the loan options available and the interest rate you qualify for. A larger down payment reduces the loan amount and can lower your monthly payments.

3. Loan Term: The loan term refers to the duration of the loan, typically ranging from 15 to 30 years. A shorter loan term results in higher monthly payments but pays off the loan faster, while a longer loan term has lower monthly payments but extends the repayment period.

4. Interest Rate: The interest rate is the percentage of the loan amount you pay as interest over the loan term. A lower interest rate translates into lower monthly payments and overall loan costs.

5. Borrower Goals: Consider your long-term financial goals and the type of property you are financing. If you plan to stay in the property for a long time, a fixed-rate mortgage may be ideal. If you anticipate moving shortly, an adjustable-rate mortgage with a lower initial rate might be suitable.

Consulting with a Mortgage Specialist

Given the complexities of real estate financing, consulting with a mortgage specialist is highly recommended. Mortgage specialists can assess your financial situation, evaluate your options, and guide you toward the loan that aligns with your specific needs and goals. They can also provide personalized advice on interest rates, down payment strategies, and other aspects of the mortgage process.

In conclusion, understanding the different types of real estate loans and seeking guidance from a mortgage specialist are crucial steps in securing the right financing for your real estate endeavors. By making informed decisions and choosing the loan that best fits your financial situation, you can embark on your real estate journey with confidence and achieve your homeownership aspirations.

6.2. Qualifying for a mortgage

Qualifying for a mortgage is a crucial step in the home-buying process. It involves demonstrating to lenders that you have the financial capacity and creditworthiness to repay the loan. Understanding the mortgage qualification process and taking proactive measures to improve your financial standing can significantly increase your chances of securing a mortgage.

Essential Creditworthiness Factors

Lenders assess your creditworthiness based on various factors, including:

1. Credit Score: Credit score is a crucial factor that lenders consider when assessing your creditworthiness and determining your eligibility for loans, including mortgages. It is a numerical representation of your credit history, indicating your ability to manage debt responsibly. A good credit score typically ranges from 700 to 800 or higher.

Lenders use credit scores as a standard way to evaluate borrowers because they provide a consistent and objective measure of creditworthiness. A high credit score indicates that you have a history of making timely payments, maintaining low credit balances, and keeping your financial obligations in good standing. This pattern suggests a lower risk of defaulting on a mortgage, making you a more desirable borrower to lenders.

Your credit score directly influences the terms and interest rates offered on mortgages. A higher credit score typically translates into lower interest rates and better loan terms, such as lower down payment requirements and more flexible repayment options. This can result in significant savings over the life of the mortgage.

Several factors contribute to your credit score, including:

a. Payment History: This is the most critical factor, accounting for 35% of your credit score. It reflects your track record of making timely payments on credit cards, loans, and other financial obligations.

b. Credit Utilization: Credit utilization refers to the percentage of your available credit that you are using. Lenders prefer borrowers who keep their credit utilization low, typically below 30%.

c. Length of Credit History: The longer your credit history, the more data lenders have to assess your creditworthiness. A longer credit history generally indicates a more established credit pattern and can positively impact your score.

d. Credit Mix: Lenders prefer borrowers with a mix of credit types, such as credit cards, installment loans, and mortgages. This demonstrates your ability to manage different types of credit responsibly.

e. New Credit Inquiries: When you apply for new credit, lenders make a hard inquiry on your credit report, which can temporarily lower your score. Multiple hard inquiries in a short period can raise concerns about your credit-seeking behavior.

To maintain a good credit score and improve your chances of qualifying for a mortgage with favorable terms, consider the following practices:

a. Make Timely Payments: Paying your bills on time is the most important factor in maintaining a good credit score. Late payments can significantly damage your score and make it difficult to qualify for loans.

b. Keep Credit Utilization Low: Aim to keep your credit utilization below 30%. This means using only a small portion of your available credit and paying off your balances regularly.

c. Avoid Opening New Credit Accounts: Avoid applying for new credit cards or loans unless necessary. Multiple hard inquiries in a short period can negatively impact your credit score.

d. Monitor Your Credit Report Regularly: Review your credit report from all three major credit bureaus (Experian, Equifax, and TransUnion) regularly to identify any errors or inaccuracies. Dispute any discrepancies promptly to ensure your score accurately reflects your credit history.

e. Consider Credit Repair Services: If your credit score is severely damaged, consider seeking assistance from a reputable credit repair service. They can help you identify and address negative items on your credit report and develop a plan to improve your score.

By maintaining a good credit score, you can enhance your financial standing, increase your chances of qualifying for favorable mortgage terms, and achieve your homeownership goals. Remember, your credit score is a reflection of your financial responsibility and can have a significant impact on your financial future.

2. Debt-to-Income Ratio (DTI): Debt-to-income ratio (DTI) is a crucial factor that lenders consider when assessing your creditworthiness and determining your eligibility for a mortgage. It measures your monthly debt obligations relative to your gross monthly income, providing insights into your ability to manage existing debt and repay a new loan.

To calculate your DTI, divide your total monthly debt payments by your gross monthly income. Your gross monthly income is the amount of money you earn before taxes and other deductions. Total monthly debt payments include mortgage payments, car loans, student loans, credit card payments, and any other regular debt obligations.

Lenders typically have DTI thresholds that they consider acceptable for borrowers. A lower DTI indicates that you have more income available to cover your debt payments, making you a less risky borrower. Generally, lenders prefer a DTI below 43%, although some may accept ratios as high as 50% for exceptional borrowers.

Your DTI plays a significant role in determining the interest rate and loan terms you qualify for. A lower DTI typically translates into lower interest rates and better loan terms, such as a lower down payment requirement. Conversely, a higher DTI may result in higher interest rates, stricter loan terms, or even denial of your mortgage application.

If you are considering purchasing a home and have concerns about your DTI, there are steps you can take to improve your chances of qualifying for a mortgage:

- Reduce Existing Debt: Pay down high-interest debt, such as credit cards, to lower your monthly payments and improve your DTI.
- Increase Income: Explore opportunities for promotions, salary increases, or additional income streams to boost your monthly income.
- Negotiate Debt Payments: Contact your creditors and inquire about potential debt consolidation or payment plan options that could reduce your monthly obligations.

- Choose a Longer Loan Term: A longer loan term can lower your monthly payments, but it will result in paying more interest over the life of the loan.
- Consider a Co-Signer: If your DTI is still too high, consider getting a co-signer with a strong credit history and income to increase your chances of approval.

A mortgage specialist can provide personalized advice and tailored strategies to improve your DTI and increase your chances of securing a favorable mortgage. They can help you create a plan to address any debt issues, manage your debt effectively, and maximize your income potential.

In conclusion, the Debt-to-income ratio is a critical factor in the mortgage qualification process. Understanding the impact of DTI and taking proactive steps to manage your debt can significantly enhance your chances of securing a mortgage and achieving your homeownership goals.

3. Employment History: Employment history is a crucial factor that lenders consider when assessing your creditworthiness for a mortgage. It provides insights into your financial stability, income consistency, and ability to repay the loan. A strong employment history demonstrates to lenders that you are a reliable borrower with a consistent source of income, which reduces the perceived risk associated with lending you money.

Lenders view employment history as a key indicator of your ability to make consistent mortgage payments. They typically want to see a stable employment history, ideally with at least two years of consistent employment in the same field or industry. This demonstrates that you have a reliable source of income and are likely to maintain that income in the future.

When evaluating your employment history, lenders typically consider the following factors:

a. Duration of Employment: A longer employment history is generally viewed more favorably. Lenders prefer to see borrowers who have been with their current employer for at least two years, as this indicates stability and reduces the risk of job loss or income disruption.

b. Job Stability: A consistent job history with minimal job hopping demonstrates your reliability and commitment to your career. Lenders are more likely to approve a mortgage for someone who has a track record of staying with their employers.

c. Industry and Occupation: The type of industry and occupation you work in can also influence lenders' assessment of your employment history. Some industries or occupations may be considered more stable or have higher earning potential, making borrowers in those fields more attractive to lenders.

d. Employer Reputation: The reputation of your employer can also play a role in lenders' evaluation. A well-established and reputable company with a strong financial standing may enhance your creditworthiness.

e. Income Levels: Lenders will also consider your income level and its consistency. A higher and consistent income demonstrates your ability to afford the mortgage payments and reduces the risk of delinquency.

If your employment history is not as strong as you would like, there are steps you can take to improve it and make yourself a more attractive borrower to lenders:

a. Maintain Stable Employment: Avoiding job hopping and staying with your current employer for as long as possible is crucial for demonstrating stability and reliability.

b. Choose a Stable Industry: Consider seeking employment in industries that are generally considered stable and have a strong outlook for future growth.

c. Document Your Achievements: Keep a record of your accomplishments and contributions at work. This can showcase your value as an employee and your potential for future earnings.

d. Explain Employment Gaps: If you have gaps in your employment history, be prepared to provide clear explanations to lenders. Address any extenuating circumstances or reasons for job changes.

e. Seek Temporary Employment: If you are currently unemployed, consider taking on temporary work to demonstrate your willingness to work and your ability to maintain a steady income.

In conclusion, employment history plays a significant role in lenders' assessment of your creditworthiness for a mortgage. By maintaining a stable employment history, choosing a stable industry, and documenting your achievements, you can increase your chances of securing a mortgage and achieving your homeownership goals. If your employment history is not ideal, take steps to improve it and provide clear explanations for any gaps or changes. Remember, a strong employment history is a valuable asset in the mortgage qualification process.

4. Down Payment: Down payment is one of the key factors that lenders consider when assessing your creditworthiness and determining your eligibility for a mortgage. It represents a significant upfront payment you make towards the purchase price of a property, typically ranging from 3% to 20% of the total cost. A larger down payment demonstrates to lenders your financial capacity, commitment to the purchase, and ability to manage a mortgage loan.

Lenders view a large down payment favorably for several reasons:

- Reduced Loan Amount: A larger down payment reduces the amount of money you need to borrow, lowering the overall loan amount and the associated interest payments over the loan term. This translates into lower monthly mortgage payments and a shorter repayment period.
- Reduced Risk for Lenders: A substantial down payment indicates that you have a vested interest in the property and are less likely to default on the loan. This reduces the lender's risk and makes you a more attractive borrower.
- Equity Building: A larger down payment translates into immediate equity in the property, providing you with a financial cushion and potentially enhancing the value of your investment.
- Eliminating PMI: Private mortgage insurance (PMI) is typically required for conventional loans when the down payment is less than 20% of the purchase price. PMI protects the lender in case of default, but it adds to your monthly mortgage payments. A down payment of 20% or more can eliminate the need for PMI, saving you money over the loan term.

Saving for a down payment requires consistent effort and financial discipline. Here are some effective strategies to consider:

a. Set Realistic Goals: Determine the down payment amount you need based on the property you are considering. Set realistic savings goals and establish a timeline to achieve them.

b. Create a Budget: Develop a detailed budget that accounts for your income, expenses, and savings goals. Identify areas where you can cut back on spending and allocate more funds toward your down payment.

c. Automate Savings: Set up automatic transfers from your checking account to a dedicated savings account. This ensures that you consistently contribute to your down payment savings without having to manually transfer funds.

d. Consider Additional Income Sources: Explore opportunities to generate additional income. This could involve taking on a side hustle, selling unused items, or monetizing your hobbies.

e. Seek Financial Assistance: If you are facing difficulty saving for a down payment, consider seeking financial assistance from family members or exploring down payment assistance programs offered by government agencies or non-profit organizations.

In summary, a substantial down payment plays a crucial role in demonstrating your creditworthiness and improving your chances of securing a mortgage with favorable terms. By implementing effective savings strategies and exploring additional income sources, you can achieve your down payment goals and lay the foundation for successful homeownership.

5. Asset Reserves: Asset reserves are financial resources that you have available beyond your income. These reserves can include savings accounts, checking accounts, investment portfolios, retirement funds, and equity in other properties. Lenders consider asset reserves when evaluating your mortgage application because they provide a safety net in case you experience unexpected financial setbacks or loss of income.

Asset reserves play a crucial role in your mortgage qualification for several reasons:

a. Demonstrate Financial Stability: Having adequate asset reserves indicates to lenders that you have the financial stability to manage your mortgage payments even if your income fluctuates or you encounter financial challenges.

b. Provide a Cushion for Unexpected Expenses: Asset reserves can serve as a buffer to cover unexpected expenses, such as medical bills, car repairs, or home maintenance issues. This helps lenders assess your ability to make consistent mortgage payments even in the face of unforeseen circumstances.

c. Reduce Reliance on Debt: Strong asset reserves can reduce your reliance on debt to meet your financial needs. This demonstrates to lenders that you are not overly reliant on credit and have a solid financial foundation.

d. Signal Commitment to the Purchase: A healthy level of asset reserves can signal to lenders that you are committed to the home purchase and have the financial means to maintain the property.

Lenders typically look for borrowers who have asset reserves equivalent to at least three to six months of living expenses. This provides them with assurance that you can cover your essential expenses if you experience a temporary loss of income.

If you are considering purchasing a home and want to strengthen your asset reserves, consider these strategies:

a. Create a Budget: Develop a detailed budget to track your income and expenses. Identify areas where you can cut back on spending and allocate those savings towards building your asset reserves.

b. Automate Savings: Set up automatic transfers from your checking account to a savings account to ensure you are consistently saving a portion of your income.

c. Increase Your Income: Explore opportunities to increase your income, such as taking on additional work, seeking a promotion, or starting a side hustle. This can help you save more money faster.

d. Invest Wisely: Consider investing a portion of your savings in low-risk, diversified investments to grow your asset reserves over time.

e. Manage Debt Effectively: Prioritize paying down high-interest debt, such as credit cards, to reduce your overall debt burden and free up more funds for savings.

f. Seek Professional Guidance: Consult with a financial advisor to develop a personalized plan for building asset reserves and achieving your financial goals.

Asset reserves play a significant role in determining your creditworthiness and your ability to qualify for a mortgage. By building a solid foundation of asset reserves, you can demonstrate your financial stability, reduce your reliance on debt, and increase your chances of securing a favorable mortgage. Remember, financial planning and proactive measures can significantly impact your mortgage qualification and overall financial well-being.

Improving Your Mortgage Qualification

If you are considering purchasing a home and have concerns about your mortgage qualification, there are steps you can take to improve your chances:

1. Check Your Credit Report: Obtain your credit report from one of the three major credit bureaus (Experian, Equifax, or TransUnion) to review your credit history and identify any errors or inaccuracies. Dispute any discrepancies with the credit bureaus to ensure your credit score accurately reflects your payment history.

2. Pay Down Debts: Reducing your existing debt obligations can lower your DTI and make you a more attractive borrower to lenders. Prioritize paying off high-interest debt, such as credit cards, to maximize the impact on your DTI.

3. Increase Your Income: Increasing your income can make you a more qualified borrower by demonstrating your ability to afford the mortgage payments. Explore opportunities for promotions, salary increases, or additional income streams.

4. Save for a Larger Down Payment: A larger down payment reduces the loan amount and lowers your monthly payments. Aim to save at least 20% of the purchase price, as this will typically eliminate the need for private mortgage insurance (PMI) and potentially secure better interest rates.

5. Maintain a Stable Employment History: Consistent employment demonstrates your financial stability and ability

to repay the loan. Avoid job hopping and maintaining a steady work record will enhance your mortgage application.

6. Seek Professional Guidance: Consulting with a mortgage specialist or financial advisor can provide personalized advice and tailored strategies to improve your mortgage qualification. They can help you create a plan to address any credit issues, manage your debt effectively, and increase your chances of securing a favorable mortgage.

Qualifying for a mortgage is a significant milestone in the homebuying process. By understanding the factors that influence mortgage qualification and taking proactive steps to improve your financial standing, you can significantly increase your chances of securing a mortgage and achieving your dream of homeownership.

6.3. Negotiating the best interest rate and terms

Securing a mortgage is a crucial step in the home-buying process, and negotiating the best interest rate and terms can significantly impact your overall financial costs and the affordability of your new home. Effective negotiation strategies can help you secure favorable terms and minimize the financial burden of your mortgage.

Before engaging in negotiations, it's essential to understand the key components of mortgage interest rates and terms:

1. Interest Rate: The interest rate is the percentage of the loan amount you pay as interest over the loan term. A lower interest rate translates into lower monthly payments and overall loan costs.

2. Loan Term: The loan term refers to the duration of the loan, typically ranging from 15 to 30 years. A shorter loan term

results in higher monthly payments but pays off the loan faster, while a longer loan term has lower monthly payments but extends the repayment period.

3. Points: Points are upfront fees paid to the lender, typically expressed as a percentage of the loan amount. One point equals 1% of the loan amount. Points can be used to lower the interest rate, but it's important to evaluate whether the savings in interest outweigh the upfront cost of points.

4. Annual Percentage Rate (APR): The APR represents the total cost of borrowing, including the interest rate, points, and other fees, expressed as an annual percentage. The APR provides a more comprehensive picture of the true cost of the loan.

Negotiation Strategies for Favorable Interest Rates and Terms

1. Shop Around and Compare Rates: Obtain pre-approvals from multiple lenders to compare interest rates and terms. This will give you a benchmark to negotiate from and identify the most competitive offers.

2. Highlight Your Creditworthiness: Emphasize your strong credit score, stable employment history, and sufficient down payment to demonstrate your ability to repay the loan responsibly. This can increase your bargaining power and encourage lenders to offer better terms.

3. Consider Alternative Financing Options: Explore alternative financing options, such as credit unions or online lenders, which may offer lower interest rates or more flexible terms.

4. Negotiate Points Strategically: If you choose to pay points to lower the interest rate, negotiate the number of points

carefully. Ensure the savings in interest outweigh the upfront cost of points.

5. Consider Non-Monetary Terms: In addition to interest rates, negotiate other aspects of the loan, such as prepayment penalties, late fees, and the ability to make additional payments without penalty.

6. Seek Professional Guidance: Consult with a mortgage specialist or financial advisor to assist you in navigating the negotiation process and securing the best possible terms for your mortgage.

Additional Tips for Successful Negotiation

1. Be Prepared: Gather all relevant financial documents, including your credit report, income verification, and asset statements, to demonstrate your financial standing to lenders.
2. Be Confident and Assertive: Communicate your goals clearly and confidently. Be prepared to negotiate, but don't settle for terms that are not in your best interests.
3. Be Patient: Negotiations may take time. Don't rush into a decision; allow time to gather information, compare offers, and make informed choices.
4. Be Willing to Walk Away: If you are not satisfied with the terms offered, be prepared to walk away from the negotiation. This demonstrates your seriousness and may encourage lenders to improve their offer.

Negotiating the best interest rate and terms for your mortgage requires a combination of preparation, knowledge, and effective communication. By understanding the factors that influence interest rates and terms, employing strategic negotiation techniques, and seeking professional guidance, you can increase your chances of securing a favorable mortgage that aligns with your financial goals and aspirations.

Chapter 7: Buying a Home as a Woman

7.1. Finding the right home for your needs and budget

Finding the right home is a crucial decision that requires careful consideration of your needs, preferences, and budget. As a woman, there may be additional factors to consider, such as safety, security, and proximity to amenities that cater to your lifestyle.

Identifying Your Needs and Priorities

Before embarking on your home search, it's essential to clearly define your needs and priorities. Consider the following questions:

1. Property Type: What type of property suits your lifestyle? Do you prefer a single-family home, a condominium, or a townhome? Each type offers different advantages and considerations, such as privacy, maintenance responsibilities, and homeowner association fees.

2. Location: Where do you want to live? Consider factors like proximity to work, schools, family, and amenities that are important to you. Evaluate the neighborhoods that appeal to you and assess their safety, community vibe, and access to essential services.

3. Size and Layout: How much space do you need? Consider the number of bedrooms, bathrooms, and living areas required for your current and future needs. Think about the layout that suits your lifestyle, ensuring it provides ample space for both privacy and shared living.

4. Budget: Determine your realistic budget, considering the purchase price, closing costs, ongoing mortgage expenses,

potential renovations, and property taxes. Consult with a mortgage specialist to understand your pre-approval and the financial implications of different property options.

5. Special Considerations: As a woman, you may have additional considerations, such as safety features, well-lit surroundings, and proximity to public transportation or police stations. Prioritize your safety and security when selecting a neighborhood and evaluating potential homes.

Research and Exploration

Once you have a clear understanding of your needs and priorities, start your research and exploration. Utilize online real estate platforms, visit open houses, and connect with real estate agents who specialize in your desired area and property type.

1. Online Searches: Utilize online resources like Zillow, Trulia, and Realtor.com to browse properties, view photos, and gather information about neighborhoods and amenities.

2. Open Houses: Attend open houses to get a firsthand look at potential homes, assess their condition, and experience the layout and flow of the property.

3. Real Estate Agents: Consult with experienced real estate agents who can provide personalized guidance, navigate the local market, and help you find properties that align with your specific criteria.

Evaluating Potential Homes

When evaluating potential homes, consider the following aspects:

1. Condition and Maintenance: Assess the overall condition of the property, including the roof, foundation, plumbing, electrical system, and any necessary repairs or renovations.

2. Functionality and Layout: Evaluate the functionality and layout of the home, ensuring it meets your needs in terms of space, storage, and flow. Consider the size and arrangement of rooms, natural light, and potential furniture placement.

3. Safety and Security: Assess the safety and security features of the home, such as alarm systems, well-lit entrances, and secure windows and doors. Consider the surrounding neighborhood and its reputation for safety.

4. Neighborhood Amenities: Evaluate the proximity and access to amenities that are important to you, such as schools, parks, grocery stores, public transportation, and recreational facilities.

5. Long-Term Value: Consider the potential long-term value of the property, factoring in its location, condition, and appreciation potential. Consult with real estate professionals to assess the property's value and growth prospects.

Making an Informed Decision

Once you have identified potential homes that meet your criteria, carefully evaluate your options and seek guidance from your real estate agent. Consider factors like price negotiations, contingencies, and the overall suitability of each property for your needs and lifestyle.

1. Price Negotiations: Prepare to negotiate the purchase price based on your evaluation of the property's value and comparable sales in the area.

2. Contingencies: Consider including contingencies in your offer, such as inspections, appraisals, and financing approvals, to protect your interests before closing the deal.

3. Informed Decision: Make an informed decision based on your comprehensive evaluation, taking into account your needs, preferences, budget, and long-term goals.

Remember, finding the right home is a journey, not a race. Take your time, do your research, and trust your instincts to find the property that truly aligns with your aspirations and lifestyle.

7.2. Making an offer

Making an offer on a home is a crucial step in the homebuying process, especially for women who may face unique challenges and considerations. By understanding the process, preparing effectively, and negotiating confidently, women can navigate this stage successfully and increase their chances of securing their dream home.

The Offer Process

An offer to purchase a home is a formal proposal made by the buyer to the seller, outlining the terms and conditions of the transaction. It typically includes the following elements:

1. Property Identification: Identify the property by its address, legal description, and any other relevant identifiers.

2. Purchase Price: Specify the amount the buyer is willing to pay for the property. This price should be based on market research, comparable sales, and the buyer's financial capacity.

3. Closing Date: Propose a date when the transaction is expected to be finalized and the property ownership transferred.

4. Earnest Money Deposit: Include an earnest money deposit, a refundable sum of money that demonstrates the buyer's seriousness and commitment to the purchase.

5. Contingencies: Outline any contingencies that may affect the purchase, such as a home inspection contingency or a financing contingency.

Preparing to Make an Offer

Before making an offer, it is essential to be well-prepared:

1. Secure Pre-Approval: Obtain pre-approval for a mortgage from a trusted lender. This demonstrates your financial ability to purchase the property and helps you understand your borrowing capacity.

2. Conduct Thorough Research: Research the property, the neighborhood, and comparable sales to determine a fair market value. Consider factors like property condition, amenities, and recent renovations.

3. Engage a Real Estate Agent: Partner with a knowledgeable and experienced real estate agent who understands the local market and can represent your best interests throughout the process.

4. Understand Contingencies: Familiarize yourself with common contingencies, such as home inspection, financing, and appraisal contingencies, and determine which ones are important for your transaction.

5. Review the Purchase Agreement: Carefully review the purchase agreement before signing, ensuring you understand all the terms, conditions, and contingencies.

Negotiating Effectively

Negotiation is an integral part of the offer process. Here are some tips for effective negotiation:

1. Set Clear Goals: Determine your negotiating goals and priorities, considering your budget, desired closing date, and any specific needs or concerns.

2. Communicate Clearly: Express your goals and concerns clearly and professionally to the seller's agent. Maintain open communication and be willing to compromise to reach a mutually agreeable outcome.

3. Be Prepared to Walk Away: Have the courage to walk away from the negotiation if the terms are not in your best interests. This demonstrates your commitment to your goals and willingness to find a suitable property.

4. Consider the Seller's Perspective: Understand the seller's perspective and their motivations for selling. This can help you approach negotiations with empathy and find a solution that benefits both parties.

5. Seek Professional Guidance: If negotiations become complex or you feel unsure, consult with your real estate agent or an attorney for expert advice and support.

Additional Considerations for Women

Women may face unique challenges when making an offer on a home:

1. Gender Stereotypes: Women may encounter gender stereotypes that underestimate their financial capabilities or

knowledge of real estate. Be prepared to assert your expertise and confidence throughout the process.

2. Financial Independence: Women may have different financial considerations, such as managing household finances, saving for retirement, or planning for childcare. Ensure your offer aligns with your long-term financial goals.

3. Safety and Security: Women may have additional safety and security concerns when considering a property. Evaluate the neighborhood, access to amenities, and potential security measures.

4. Seeking Support: Surround yourself with a supportive team of professionals, including a real estate agent, financial advisor, and attorney, who can advocate for your interests and provide guidance throughout the homebuying process.

In conclusion, making an offer on a home is an exciting and empowering step towards homeownership. By understanding the offer process, preparing effectively, negotiating confidently, and considering unique challenges faced by women, you can increase your chances of securing the home of your dreams and achieving your real estate goals.

7.3. Closing on your home

Closing on a home is a significant milestone in the homebuying process, marking the culmination of months of planning, searching, and negotiating. For women embarking on this journey, understanding the closing process and its nuances is crucial to ensuring a smooth and successful transaction.

The Pre-Closing Phase: Ensuring a Smooth Closing

The pre-closing phase involves finalizing paperwork, securing financing, and preparing for the closing day. Here are some key steps to navigate this phase effectively:

1. Review and Finalize Documents: Carefully review all closing documents, including the purchase agreement, title reports, and mortgage loan documents, to ensure accuracy and understanding. Ask questions and seek clarification if necessary.

2. Secure Financing: Confirm your mortgage loan approval and ensure all financing arrangements are in place. Provide any required documentation promptly and address any outstanding issues with your lender.

3. Schedule Home Inspection: Schedule a thorough home inspection to assess the property's condition and identify any potential repairs or maintenance needs. Discuss any concerns with your agent and negotiate with the seller as needed.

4. Arrange Insurance: Obtain homeowner's insurance coverage to protect your investment and meet your lender's requirements. Compare rates and coverage options from different insurers.

5. Plan for Closing Costs: Gather funds to cover closing costs, which typically include appraisal fees, title insurance, lender fees, prepaid property taxes, and homeowner's insurance premiums.

Closing Day: Finalizing the Purchase

Closing day is the culmination of the homebuying process, where you officially transfer ownership of the property. Here are some key steps to ensure a smooth closing:

1. Arrive Early and Prepared: Arrive at the closing meeting early with all necessary documents, including your identification, proof of insurance, and closing funds.

2. Review and Sign Documents: Carefully review all closing documents, including the final title report, loan documents, and closing disclosure statement. Ask questions if needed and sign documents as instructed.

4. Transfer Ownership: Sign the title transfer documents, officially transferring ownership of the property to your name.

5. Pay Closing Costs: Provide your closing funds to cover closing costs, typically in the form of a cashier's check or wire transfer.

6. Receive Keys and Insurance Policies: Receive your keys to the property and copies of your homeowner's insurance policies.

Additional Considerations for Women Homebuyers

As a woman embarking on the homebuying journey, consider these additional tips:

1. Educate Yourself: Familiarize yourself with the home buying process, mortgage options, and closing procedures. Attend workshops, and seminars, or consult with a real estate professional to gain knowledge and confidence.

2. Seek Support: Surround yourself with a supportive network, including a trusted real estate agent, financial advisor, or experienced homeowner. Their guidance can be invaluable throughout the process.

3. Negotiate Confidently: Approach negotiations with confidence and assertiveness. Research market values,

comparable sales, and potential concessions to strengthen your negotiating position.

4. Protect Yourself: Be mindful of potential scams or unethical practices. Stay informed, ask questions, and seek professional advice when necessary.

5. Advocate for Yourself: Don't hesitate to ask questions, seek clarifications, and advocate for your best interests. Your assertiveness will ensure a fair and transparent transaction.

Closing on a home is a significant achievement, and for women, it represents an empowering step toward financial stability and independence. By understanding the closing process, preparing thoroughly, and advocating for your interests, you can navigate this exciting milestone with confidence and successfully secure your dream home.

Chapter 8: Selling Your Home as a Woman

8.1. Preparing your home for sale

Preparing your home for sale is a crucial step in the process of selling your property successfully. By taking the time to make your home appealing to potential buyers, you can increase your chances of getting the best possible price and selling your home quickly.

Enhancing Curb Appeal

Curb appeal refers to the first impression that your home makes on potential buyers as they drive by. A well-maintained exterior can significantly impact buyer interest and set the stage for a positive overall impression. Here are some key tips for enhancing curb appeal:

1. Landscaping: Keep your lawn mowed, edged, and free of weeds. Plant colorful flowers and shrubs to add visual interest and enhance the overall aesthetic.

2. Exterior Maintenance: Repair any cracks or peeling paint on the exterior walls and trim. Replace any damaged siding or shingles.

3. Front Door: Paint your front door in a welcoming color and replace any worn-out hardware. Ensure the door opens and closes smoothly.

4. Porch and Walkway: Sweep or power wash your porch and walkway to remove dirt and debris. Add potted plants or flowers to brighten up the space.

5. Garage Door: Paint or clean your garage door to make it look fresh and inviting. Check that the garage door opener is functioning properly.

Decluttering and Depersonalizing

Decluttering and depersonalizing your home are essential steps to make it appear spacious, clean, and move-in ready. A cluttered or overly personalized home can make it difficult for potential buyers to envision themselves living in the space.

1. Declutter: Remove excess furniture, personal belongings, and clutter from all rooms. This will create a more spacious and inviting feel.

2. Pack Away Personal Items: Pack away personal items such as family photos, souvenirs, and collections. These items can distract buyers from the overall features of the home.

3. Neutralize Décor: Consider replacing brightly colored or patterned décor with neutral tones. Neutral colors create a sense of calm and make the home feel more spacious.

4. Staging: Consider staging your home professionally or using staging techniques to enhance the appeal of each room. Staging can help buyers visualize the potential of the space.

Deep Cleaning and Repairs

A thorough cleaning and attention to minor repairs can significantly improve the overall presentation of your home. A clean and well-maintained home conveys a sense of care and attention to detail.

1. Deep Clean: Deep clean all rooms, including carpets, upholstery, and hard surfaces. Pay attention to areas that are often overlooked, such as baseboards, vents, and appliances.

2. Minor Repairs: Address any minor repairs that could detract from the overall impression of your home. Fix leaky faucets,

replace cracked tiles, and repair any loose or damaged doorknobs.

3. Kitchens and Bathrooms: Pay particular attention to kitchens and bathrooms, as these are high-impact areas for buyers. Ensure countertops are clean, appliances are functioning properly, and plumbing fixtures are free of leaks or rust.

4. Fresh Paint: Consider repainting walls in neutral colors to brighten up the space and create a fresh, modern feel.

5. Lighting: Ensure all rooms have adequate lighting, both natural and artificial. Bright and well-lit spaces make the home feel more welcoming and inviting.

Professional Photography and Marketing

High-quality photography and effective marketing are essential to showcase your home to potential buyers. Professional photography can capture the best features of your home and attract more interest.

1. Professional Photography: Hire a professional photographer to take high-quality images of your home. These photos will be used for online listings and marketing materials.

2. Marketing Strategy: Develop a comprehensive marketing strategy that targets potential buyers in your area. This may include online listings, social media campaigns, and print advertising.

3. Highlight Unique Features: Emphasize any unique features or amenities that set your home apart from others in the area. This could include a home office, a spacious backyard, or a renovated kitchen.

4. Target Your Audience: Tailor your marketing materials to the specific needs and preferences of potential buyers in your target demographic.

By following these tips, you can effectively prepare your home for sale and increase your chances of achieving your desired selling price and timeline. Remember, first impressions matter and a well-presented home will attract more buyers and potentially lead to a quick and successful sale.

8.2. Pricing your home correctly

Pricing your home correctly is a crucial step in the selling process, as it significantly impacts the overall success of your transaction. Setting the right price can attract potential buyers, generate interest, and ultimately lead to a successful sale. Here's an in-depth discussion on pricing your home correctly, tailored specifically for women homeowners:

Factors Influencing Home Pricing

Several factors influence the appropriate asking price for your home. These include:

1. Location: Location is one of the most crucial factors that influence the pricing of your home, and it holds particular significance for women homeowners. Women often face unique challenges and considerations when it comes to choosing a neighborhood and understanding the impact of location on their home's value.

The location of your home plays a significant role in its overall value and appeal to potential buyers. Properties in desirable neighborhoods with proximity to amenities, schools, and transportation hubs typically command higher prices. Here's a breakdown of how location affects home value:

a. Neighborhood Quality: The overall quality and reputation of the neighborhood where your home is situated significantly impacts its value. Homes in safe, well-maintained neighborhoods with a strong sense of community tend to be more desirable and command higher prices.

b. Proximity to Amenities: Access to essential amenities, such as grocery stores, parks, recreational facilities, and entertainment options, enhances a home's value. Properties close to these amenities offer convenience and lifestyle benefits, making them more attractive to potential buyers.

c. School Quality: The quality of local schools is a major factor for families with school-aged children. Homes within the boundaries of reputable school districts typically command higher prices due to the perceived educational advantages they offer.

d. Transportation Access: Proximity to public transportation options, such as bus stops, train stations, or subway lines, increases a home's value, especially in urban areas. Easy access to transportation provides convenience and commuting options for potential buyers.

e. Crime Rates: Lower crime rates and a sense of safety contribute to higher home values. Properties in neighborhoods with low crime rates are more desirable and command higher prices due to the perceived safety and livability they offer.

Women homeowners may face unique considerations when it comes to location and home value. Here are some factors to consider:

a) Safety and Security: Women often prioritize safety and security when choosing a neighborhood. Homes in well-lit areas with low crime rates and a strong sense of community are particularly appealing to women homeowners.

b) Proximity to Work and Support Networks: Women often balance multiple roles, including work, family, and personal commitments. Choosing a location that is close to work, daycare facilities and support networks can be a priority for women homeowners.

c) Accessibility and Walkability: Women may value neighborhoods that offer walkability, access to public transportation, and bike-friendly infrastructure. This allows for convenient commuting, errands, and leisure activities without relying solely on cars.

d) Amenities for Families and Children: Women with families may prioritize neighborhoods with parks, playgrounds, family-friendly activities, and proximity to childcare options. These amenities enhance the livability and appeal of families with children.

e) Diversity and Inclusion: Women may value neighborhoods that are diverse, inclusive, and welcoming to all. A sense of belonging and acceptance can be a significant factor in choosing a community.

To navigate location considerations effectively, women homeowners can follow these strategies:

a. Identify Personal Priorities: Clearly define your priorities and what you value most in a neighborhood. Consider factors like safety, convenience, amenities, and access to support networks.

b. Conduct Thorough Research: Research different neighborhoods and communities, paying attention to crime rates, school quality, proximity to amenities, and transportation options. Utilize online resources, community forums, and consultations with real estate professionals to gather information.

c. Seek Recommendations: Network with friends, family, colleagues, or community members who live in areas you're considering. Their insights and experiences can provide valuable perspectives on the livability and suitability of different neighborhoods.

d. Visit Neighborhoods in Person: Personally visit potential neighborhoods to experience the atmosphere, assess the quality of life, and evaluate the overall safety and appeal of the community.

e. Consult with Experienced Professionals: Collaborate with experienced real estate agents who have a strong understanding of the local market and the unique needs of women homeowners. They can provide valuable insights, guide you through the home search process, and help you find a neighborhood that aligns with your priorities and preferences.

By carefully considering the impact of location on home value and prioritizing your personal needs, women homeowners can make informed decisions about neighborhood selection and maximize the value of their properties.

2. Condition and Features: Condition and features play a significant role in determining the value of a home, and women homeowners should pay particular attention to these aspects when pricing their properties.

The overall condition of a home significantly impacts its value. A well-maintained, updated, and move-in-ready property commands a higher price compared to a home that requires substantial repairs or renovations. Potential buyers are willing to pay more for a home that is in good condition, as it reduces their risk of incurring unexpected expenses and ensures a comfortable living environment.

Several condition-related factors influence home value, including:

a. Structural Integrity: The structural integrity of the home, including the foundation, roof, and framing, is crucial. Buyers are willing to pay more for a home with a sound structure that is free from major defects.

b. Interior Condition: The overall condition of the interior, including flooring, walls, ceilings, and finishes, plays a significant role in value. A well-maintained interior with modern finishes and upgrades is highly desirable to buyers.

c. Mechanical Systems: The functionality of mechanical systems, such as plumbing, electrical wiring, heating, and cooling, is essential. Buyers prefer homes with well-maintained and up-to-date mechanical systems.

d. Curb Appeal: The curb appeal, or the exterior appearance of the home, creates a first impression and influences buyer interest. A well-maintained exterior with landscaping, fresh paint, and inviting features can enhance the home's value.

Certain features can significantly increase the value of a home. These include:

a. Modern Amenities: Modern amenities, such as updated kitchens and bathrooms, energy-efficient appliances, smart home technology, and outdoor living spaces, are highly sought-after by buyers.

b. Unique Features: Unique features that differentiate the home from others in the neighborhood, such as architectural details, special rooms, or recreational amenities, can add value.

c. Energy Efficiency: Energy-efficient features, such as solar panels, double-pane windows, and high-efficiency appliances, are increasingly attractive to buyers due to their cost-saving benefits.

d. Sustainability Features: Sustainable features, such as water-saving fixtures, recycled materials, and environmentally friendly landscaping, appeal to buyers who value sustainability and eco-conscious living.

Strategies for Women Homeowners to Enhance Condition and Features

Women homeowners can employ various strategies to enhance the condition and features of their homes, thereby increasing their value:

a. Prioritize Repairs and Maintenance: Address any necessary repairs or maintenance promptly to ensure the home is in good condition. This may include fixing leaky faucets, patching cracks in walls, and maintaining landscaping.

b. Consider Modernization: Consider updating outdated finishes, such as replacing old countertops, appliances, and flooring, to enhance the home's appeal.

c. Leverage Existing Features: Highlight unique features that make the home special, such as architectural details, outdoor spaces, or recreational amenities.

d. Seek Professional Advice: Consult with interior designers or home improvement specialists for guidance on enhancing the home's condition and incorporating modern features that appeal to buyers.

In conclusion, by paying close attention to the condition and features of their homes, women homeowners can significantly increase their property's value and attract potential buyers. Investing in necessary repairs, modernizing outdated elements, and highlighting unique features can enhance the home's appeal and command a higher asking price.

3. Comparable Sales:

Comparable sales, also known as "comps," play a crucial role in determining the appropriate asking price for your home. When selling your property, understanding and analyzing comparable sales is essential for setting a competitive yet achievable price that aligns with market conditions and attracts potential buyers.

Comparable sales are recent sales of similar properties in your area that share similar characteristics to your home. These sales provide valuable insights into the current market value of your property, as they reflect what buyers are willing to pay for homes with comparable features, conditions, and locations.

Comparable sales are particularly important for women homeowners as they help ensure that their homes are priced fairly and competitively, considering the unique challenges that women may face in the real estate market. By carefully analyzing comparable sales, women homeowners can avoid underpricing their properties, which can significantly impact their financial gains from the sale.

Analyzing comparable sales effectively involves a systematic approach:

a. Identify Comparable Properties: Begin by identifying a list of recently sold properties that closely resemble your home in terms of size, style, age, condition, location, and amenities. Focus on properties that have sold within the past six months to reflect the most current market trends.

b. Gather Information: Collect detailed information about each comparable property, including the sale price, square footage, number of bedrooms and bathrooms, lot size, special features, and any relevant renovations or updates.

c. Adjust for Differences: Carefully evaluate any differences between your home and the comparable properties. For instance, if your home has a larger lot or more modern features, you may adjust the comparable sales prices upward.

d. Consider Market Trends: Assess overall market trends, including supply and demand, buyer preferences, and interest rates, as these factors can influence the value of comparable sales and your home's pricing.

e. Seek Professional Guidance: Consult with an experienced real estate agent who specializes in your area and understands the nuances of comparable sales analysis. Their expertise can help you refine your analysis and make informed decisions.

Once you have analyzed comparable sales, use the information to establish a fair and realistic asking price for your home. Consider the following guidelines:

a. Comparative Analysis: Compare the selling prices of comparable properties to your home's characteristics, adjusting for any notable differences.

b. Market Range: Determine the price range within which comparable properties have sold. Aim to set your asking price within this range to attract potential buyers.

c. Professional Input: Seek feedback from your real estate agent on your proposed asking price. They can provide insights based on their experience and knowledge of the local market.

d. Consider Negotiation: Be prepared to negotiate with potential buyers. Comparable sales provide a solid foundation for negotiation but remain open to adjusting your price based on market conditions and buyer offers.

In summary, comparable sales are an invaluable tool for women homeowners in determining the appropriate asking price for their properties. By carefully analyzing comparable sales, understanding market trends, and seeking professional guidance, women homeowners can ensure they are pricing their homes competitively, maximizing their potential financial gains while navigating the complexities of the real estate market.

4. Current Market Conditions: Pricing your home correctly is a crucial decision that can significantly impact the overall success of your sale. Current market conditions play a substantial role in determining an appropriate asking price, as they influence buyer demand, competition, and overall pricing expectations. Women homeowners, like all sellers, should carefully consider the current market landscape when setting the price for their property.

Numerous factors contribute to the current market conditions, and understanding these indicators is essential for women homeowners:

a. Supply and Demand: The balance between the availability of homes for sale and the number of active buyers significantly impacts pricing. In a seller's market, where demand exceeds supply, prices tend to be higher. Conversely, in a buyer's market, where supply surpasses demand, prices may be lower or more negotiable.

b. Buyer Sentiment: The overall mood and confidence level of potential buyers influence their willingness to purchase and the prices they are prepared to pay. Positive buyer sentiment, driven by factors like economic stability, low interest rates, and job growth, can lead to increased demand and higher prices.

c. Interest Rates: Interest rates directly impact the affordability of homes, influencing buyers' purchasing power and overall demand. Lower interest rates make mortgages more affordable, increasing buyers' ability to purchase homes and potentially driving up prices.

d. Local Economic Conditions: The economic health of the area where your home is located plays a role in its value. Strong employment, business growth, and population growth contribute to a thriving real estate market, where prices tend to be higher.

e. National Economic Trends: National economic trends, such as inflation, unemployment rates, and consumer spending patterns, can indirectly affect local market conditions and influence home pricing.

Strategies for Women Homeowners to Navigate Current Market Conditions

Women homeowners can effectively navigate current market conditions by adopting these strategies:

a. Stay Informed: Keep up-to-date on local and national market trends through reputable sources, such as real estate market reports, industry publications, and consultations with experienced real estate professionals.

b. Analyze Local Data: Gather and analyze data on recent sales of comparable properties in your neighborhood. This information will provide insights into current pricing trends and allow you to set a competitive asking price.

c. Seek Professional Guidance: Consult with experienced real estate agents who have a strong understanding of the local market and the unique needs of women homeowners. Their expertise can help you navigate market complexities and determine the optimal pricing strategy for your property.

d. Consider Your Goals: Clearly define your financial goals for the sale and align your pricing strategy with these objectives. Whether you aim to maximize your profit or achieve a quick sale, your goals should guide your pricing decisions.

e. Be Flexible and Adaptable: The real estate market is dynamic, and market conditions can change rapidly. Be prepared to adjust your pricing strategy as needed based on market fluctuations, buyer feedback, and your evolving goals.

In conclusion, current market conditions play a significant role in determining the appropriate asking price for your home. By understanding the key market indicators, staying informed, seeking professional guidance, and considering your goals, women homeowners can confidently navigate current market conditions and make informed pricing decisions that align with their financial objectives and maximize the success of their home sales.

5. Professional Appraisal:

In the process of selling a home, pricing accurately is a crucial step that can significantly impact the overall success of the transaction. For women homeowners, who may face unique challenges in pricing their homes, obtaining a professional appraisal can provide an unbiased assessment of their property's value and ensure a fair asking price.

A professional appraisal is an unbiased evaluation of a property's market value conducted by a licensed appraiser. The appraiser considers various factors, including the property's condition, features, location, comparable sales, and current market conditions, to determine an objective estimate of its worth.

Why is a Professional Appraisal Important for Women Homeowners?

Women homeowners may face unique challenges in pricing their homes due to factors such as:

a. Gender Bias: Studies have shown that women may undervalue their homes compared to their male counterparts, potentially leading to lower asking prices and reduced profits.

b. Overemotional Attachment: Women may form strong emotional attachments to their homes, making it difficult to detach themselves emotionally when setting the asking price. This can lead to underpricing or overpricing of the property.

c. Lack of Experience: Women may have less experience with real estate transactions, making them more susceptible to pricing errors and potentially undervaluing their homes.

Benefits of a Professional Appraisal for Women Homeowners

A professional appraisal can provide numerous benefits for women homeowners, including:

a. Unbiased Valuation: An appraiser's objective assessment removes emotional biases and ensures that the property's value is determined based on market data and comparable sales.

b. Market Expertise: Appraisers possess in-depth knowledge of the local real estate market, enabling them to consider factors such as supply and demand, buyer preferences, and recent trends to determine a fair asking price.

c. Negotiation Confidence: An appraisal report provides women homeowners with a strong foundation for negotiating with potential buyers, ensuring they receive a fair price for their property.

d. Risk Mitigation: An accurate appraisal can help mitigate potential risks associated with overpricing or underpricing the property.

How to Obtain a Professional Appraisal

To obtain a professional appraisal, women homeowners can:

a. Contact a Licensed Appraiser: Search for licensed appraisers in their area through reputable online directories or seek recommendations from real estate professionals.

b. Schedule an Appraisal Appointment: Provide the appraiser with detailed information about the property, including its address, square footage, recent renovations, and unique features.

c. Review the Appraisal Report: Carefully review the appraisal report to understand the appraiser's methodology, valuation rationale, and comparable sales analysis.

In conclusion, for women homeowners, a professional appraisal is an invaluable tool that can empower them to make informed decisions about pricing their homes, ensuring a fair and profitable sale. By obtaining an appraisal, women homeowners can level the playing field, overcome potential biases, and maximize the value of their real estate investments.

Pricing Strategies for Women Homeowners

Women homeowners may face unique challenges in pricing their homes. To navigate these challenges effectively, consider the following strategies:

a) Conduct Thorough Research: Thoroughly research comparable sales in your area, paying close attention to the features, condition, and selling prices of similar properties. This will help you establish a realistic price range for your home.

b) Seek Guidance from Experienced Professionals: Consult with experienced real estate professionals, particularly those who have a strong understanding of the local market and the unique needs of women homeowners. Their expertise can guide you in setting a competitive yet achievable asking price.

c) Consider Emotional Attachment: While emotional attachment to your home is understandable, it's important to detach yourself emotionally when setting the asking price. Focus on objective factors, market conditions, and comparable sales to ensure you're pricing your home fairly.

d) Negotiate Confidently: Be prepared to negotiate with potential buyers. Arm yourself with market data, comparable sales, and a clear understanding of your desired selling price. Negotiate confidently and professionally to secure the best possible outcome.

Pricing Tips for a Successful Sale

To increase your chances of a successful sale, consider these additional pricing tips:

a) Price Competitively: Aim to set a price that is competitive within your local market, attracting potential buyers without leaving money on the table.

b) Consider Time of Year: Seasonality can affect buyer demand and pricing strategies. Consult with your real estate agent to determine the optimal time to list your home based on market trends and buyer activity.

c) Consider Staging: Staging your home professionally can significantly enhance its appeal to potential buyers. A well-staged home showcases its best features and creates a positive first impression.

d) Seek Feedback: Gather feedback from potential buyers and real estate professionals to evaluate your pricing strategy. Use this feedback to make informed adjustments if necessary.

Pricing your home correctly is a critical decision that can significantly impact the outcome of your sale. By understanding the factors influencing home value, adopting effective pricing strategies, and seeking guidance from experienced professionals, you can increase your chances of achieving a successful and profitable sale.

8.3. Marketing your home to potential buyers

Effectively marketing your home to potential buyers is crucial for achieving a successful sale. It involves creating a compelling narrative that showcases your home's unique features and resonates with the target audience. As a woman homeowner, you can tailor your marketing strategies to connect with potential buyers and achieve your selling goals.

Identifying Your Target Audience

Before embarking on your marketing campaign, it's essential to identify your target audience. Understanding the type of buyer, you're seeking will help you tailor your marketing efforts and attract the right potential buyers. Consider factors such as:

- Family size: Are you targeting families with children, couples, or single professionals?
- Age group: Are you targeting first-time homebuyers, downsizers, or retirees?
- Lifestyle preferences: Are you marketing your home to those seeking outdoor activities, proximity to amenities, or a quiet neighborhood?

Once you have a clear understanding of your target audience, you can tailor your marketing messages and channels to reach them effectively.

High-Quality Photography and Staging

Visual appeal plays a significant role in attracting potential buyers. Invest in high-quality professional photography that captures the essence of your home, highlighting its best features and creating a sense of warmth and invitingness. Consider staging your home to enhance its appeal and showcase its potential. Staging involves arranging furniture, adding décor, and creating a welcoming ambiance that resonates with your target audience.

Curated Online Listings

Online listings are often the first point of contact for potential buyers. Create comprehensive and engaging online listings that provide detailed information about your home, including its features, amenities, and unique selling points. Use clear and concise language, highlight the lifestyle benefits of living in your home, and optimize your listings for search engines.

Leveraging Social Media Platforms

Social media platforms offer powerful marketing tools for reaching a wider audience. Utilize social media platforms like Facebook, Instagram, and Pinterest to share captivating images and videos of your home, engage with potential buyers, and generate interest. Create targeted social media ads to reach specific demographics and interests.

Open Houses and Community Events

Host open houses to allow potential buyers to experience your home firsthand. Create a welcoming atmosphere, provide refreshments, and have knowledgeable agents or representatives available to answer questions and highlight the property's features. Participate in local community events to connect with potential buyers and network with real estate professionals.

Collaboration with Real Estate Professionals

Partner with an experienced real estate agent who specializes in your area and understands the unique needs of women homeowners. A knowledgeable agent can provide valuable guidance, develop a tailored marketing plan, and negotiate effectively on your behalf.

Tailoring Your Approach as a Woman Homeowner

As a woman homeowner, you can leverage your unique perspective and experiences to connect with potential buyers. Highlight the features that make your home specifically appealing to women, such as a well-equipped kitchen, functional family spaces, and safety features. Share your anecdotes about living in the home and the community to create a connection with potential buyers.

Effective marketing is key to a successful home sale. By understanding your target audience, creating compelling visuals, utilizing online platforms, hosting open houses, collaborating with professionals, and tailoring your approach as a woman homeowner, you can attract potential buyers, showcase your home's unique value, and achieve your selling goals.

8.4. Negotiating with buyers

Negotiating with buyers is an integral part of the home-selling process, and it can be a daunting task, especially for women homeowners. However, with preparation, knowledge, and confidence, you can navigate the negotiation process effectively and achieve a favorable outcome.

Preparation is Key

Before entering negotiations, it is essential to be well-prepared. This involves:

1. Gathering Information: Thoroughly research comparable sales in your area to understand the market value of similar properties. Gather information on recent sales, market trends, and buyer preferences to establish a realistic negotiating range.

2. Setting Clear Goals: Define your negotiation goals clearly, whether it's maximizing your profit or achieving a specific closing price. Having clear goals will guide your negotiations and help you make informed decisions.

3. Understanding Your Home's Value: Objectively assess your home's value, considering its condition, features, and location. A professional appraisal can provide an unbiased assessment of your home's fair market value.

4. Consulting with Professionals: Seek guidance from experienced real estate professionals, particularly those who specialize in representing sellers and have a strong understanding of the local market. Their expertise can help you navigate the negotiation process effectively.

Effective Negotiation Strategies

During negotiations with buyers, employ effective strategies to protect your interests and achieve your goals:

1. Set the Anchor: The first offer sets the anchor for the negotiation. Consider starting with a slightly higher price than your desired selling price to give yourself room for negotiation.

2. Active Listening: Actively listen to the buyer's concerns and proposals. Understand their perspective and consider their needs, but don't feel pressured to accept their initial offer.

3. Counter-Offer Strategically: When countering, don't jump to the buyer's offer. Counter with a price that aligns with your

goals and market data. Be prepared to negotiate multiple times until an agreement is reached.

4. Highlight Your Home's Value: Showcase the unique features and benefits of your home that make it desirable to buyers. Emphasize upgrades, renovations, and any special qualities that set your property apart.

5. Consider Contingencies: Carefully review and negotiate any contingencies, such as inspection or financing contingencies. Ensure that the contingencies are reasonable and protect your interests.

6. Maintain Composure: Negotiations can be stressful, but maintain your composure and professionalism throughout the process. Avoid emotional reactions and focus on achieving a mutually beneficial outcome.

7. Seek Professional Advice: If negotiations become complex or you feel uncomfortable, don't hesitate to seek advice from your real estate agent or attorney. They can provide guidance and protect your interests throughout the negotiation process.

Negotiating with Confidence as a Woman Homeowner

As a woman homeowner, negotiating with buyers may present additional challenges. However, you can approach negotiations with confidence by:

a) Educating Yourself: Equip yourself with knowledge about the local real estate market, negotiation techniques, and legal aspects of home sales. Attend workshops, seminars, or online courses to enhance your negotiating skills.

b) Building a Strong Support Team: Surround yourself with experienced professionals, such as a real estate agent, attorney, and financial advisor. Their expertise and support can empower you to make informed decisions and negotiate effectively.

c) Communicating Assertively: Communicate your goals and expectations clearly and assertively. Avoid being apologetic or hesitant; express your views confidently and professionally.

d) Trusting Your Instincts: Pay attention to your instincts and don't feel pressured to accept an offer that doesn't align with your goals. Trust in your ability to negotiate a fair deal.

e) Seeking Support: If you face discrimination or unfair treatment during negotiations, don't hesitate to seek support from women's organizations, real estate associations, or legal aid resources.

Negotiating with buyers is an essential aspect of the home-selling process, and it requires preparation, knowledge, and confidence. By following these strategies and approaches, women homeowners can effectively navigate negotiations, achieve favorable outcomes, and protect their interests in the home selling process. Remember, you are in control of your property and your negotiations, so approach the process with confidence and assertiveness.

Chapter 9: Investing in Real Estate

9.1. The benefits of investing in real estate

Real estate has long been considered a valuable asset class, offering a plethora of benefits to investors. From generating passive income to providing long-term wealth appreciation, real estate investments can play a significant role in achieving financial stability and building wealth over time. Here's an in-depth exploration of the key benefits of investing in real estate:

1. Passive Income Generation: One of the most compelling benefits of real estate investing is the potential to generate passive income. Through rental properties, investors can earn regular cash flow from tenants, providing a steady stream of income without active involvement in the day-to-day management of the property. This passive income can supplement or replace earned income, enhancing overall financial stability.

2. Capital Appreciation and Long-Term Wealth Creation: Real estate has historically demonstrated a strong track record of capital appreciation, meaning that the value of properties tends to increase over time. As demand for housing and commercial space continues to grow, real estate investments have the potential to generate significant long-term wealth. Investors can benefit from this appreciation by selling properties at a higher price than their original purchase cost.

3. Diversification and Inflation Hedging: Real estate can serve as a valuable diversification tool within an investment portfolio. Unlike stocks and bonds, which are directly influenced by market fluctuations, real estate tends to exhibit lower correlation, reducing overall portfolio volatility. Additionally, real estate investments can act as a hedge against inflation. As the cost of living increases, rents and property values tend to rise, protecting the purchasing power of real estate assets.

4. Tangible Asset with Tax Benefits: Real estate is a tangible asset, providing investors with a physical property that can be seen, touched, and utilized. This tangibility offers a sense of security and stability compared to intangible investments like stocks or bonds. Moreover, real estate investments offer various tax benefits, including depreciation deductions, mortgage interest deductions, and potential capital gains tax deferrals.

5. Control and Leverage: Real estate investments provide investors with a degree of control over their assets. Unlike mutual funds or ETFs, where investors relinquish control to fund managers, real estate investors have the autonomy to make decisions about property management, renovations, and potential resale. Additionally, real estate investments offer the potential for leverage, allowing investors to purchase properties using borrowed funds, magnifying potential returns.

6. Community Building and Legacy: Investing in real estate can contribute positively to communities by providing quality housing and commercial spaces. Investors can play a role in revitalizing neighborhoods, enhancing property values, and contributing to local economic development. Additionally, real estate investments can serve as a legacy, providing wealth and opportunities for future generations.

In conclusion, Real estate investments offer a multitude of benefits, including passive income generation, capital appreciation, diversification, tangibility, control, leverage, and community impact. While real estate investments, like any investment, carry inherent risks, the potential rewards make them a compelling option for investors seeking to build wealth, generate passive income, and secure a tangible asset for the future.

9.2. How to get started with real estate investing

Embarking on a journey in real estate investing can be an exciting and rewarding endeavor. Whether you aspire to generate passive income, build a long-term wealth portfolio, or simply explore new investment opportunities, real estate offers a diverse range of possibilities. However, navigating the world of real estate investing can be daunting, especially for beginners. Here's a guide on how to get started with real estate investing:

1. Define Your Investment Goals

Before embarking on your real estate investing journey, it is crucial to define your specific goals. What do you hope to achieve through real estate investing? Are you seeking immediate cash flow, long-term appreciation, or a combination of both? Establishing clear goals will guide your investment strategy and help you select the most suitable investment properties.

2. Educate Yourself and Stay Informed

Real estate investing involves a wealth of knowledge and understanding of market trends, legal aspects, and financial considerations. Dedicate time to educating yourself about various investment strategies, property types, and market dynamics. Attend workshops, seminars, or online courses to gain insights from experienced investors and industry experts.

3. Assess Your Financial Situation

Real estate investing requires a solid financial foundation. Evaluate your current financial situation, including your income, debts, and savings. Determine how much capital you can comfortably invest in real estate without straining your finances. Consider consulting with a financial advisor to assess your risk tolerance and develop a personalized investment plan.

4. Explore Different Investment Options

Real estate investing offers a variety of options, each with its own set of characteristics and risks. Familiarize yourself with different investment strategies, such as:

- Direct Ownership: Purchasing and managing physical properties, either as a landlord or for resale.
- Real Estate Investment Trusts (REITs): Investing in publicly traded companies that own and operate income-producing real estate.
- Real Estate Investment Groups (REIGs): Investing in pools of real estate managed by experienced professionals.

5. Seek Guidance from Experienced Professionals

Real estate investing can be complex and may involve legal, financial, and tax considerations. Seek guidance from experienced professionals, such as real estate agents, property managers, financial advisors, and real estate attorneys. Their expertise can help you navigate the complexities of the market, make informed decisions, and protect your interests.

6. Start Small and Build Gradually

As a beginner, it is advisable to start with smaller investments to gain experience and minimize risks. Consider investing in a single-family home or a small multifamily property before venturing into larger projects. As you gain experience and knowledge, you can gradually expand your investment portfolio.

7. Conduct Thorough Due Diligence

Before investing in any property, conduct thorough due diligence to assess its condition, potential risks, and investment potential. This may involve inspecting the property, reviewing property reports, and analyzing comparable sales in the area.

8. Manage Your Investments Effectively

Real estate investing requires active management and attention. Whether you manage the properties yourself or hire a property manager, ensure that your investments are well-maintained, tenant issues are addressed promptly, and financial records are kept accurately.

9. Stay Patient and Disciplined

Real estate investing is a long-term endeavor, and success rarely happens overnight. Practice patience, discipline, and consistency in your investment approach. Avoid impulsive decisions, stay focused on your long-term goals, and make informed choices based on sound research and analysis.

10. Continuously Learn and Adapt

The real estate market is constantly evolving, so it is essential to stay up-to-date on industry trends, emerging technologies, and regulatory changes. Continuously educate yourself, attend networking events, and seek advice from experienced investors to adapt your strategies and stay ahead of the curve.

Remember, real estate investing can be a rewarding venture, but it also involves risks and requires careful planning and execution. By following these guidelines, you can equip yourself with the knowledge, strategies, and resources to make informed decisions and embark on a successful journey in the world of real estate investing.

9.3. Different types of real estate investments

Real estate investing offers a variety of opportunities to generate wealth and build a strong financial portfolio. From purchasing rental properties to engaging in real estate crowdfunding, there are numerous investment options tailored to different risk appetites, investment goals, and levels of expertise. Understanding the different types of real estate investments can help you identify the strategies that align with your financial objectives and risk tolerance.

Traditional Real Estate Investments

Traditional real estate investments involve purchasing physical properties, such as single-family homes, multi-family apartments, commercial buildings, or land. These investments offer the potential for capital appreciation, rental income, and tax benefits.

a) Single-Family Homes: Investing in single-family homes is a popular choice for real estate investors. These properties can be rented to tenants, generating a steady stream of rental income. Additionally, single-family homes can appreciate over time, providing capital gains for investors.

b) Multi-Family Apartments: Multi-family apartments offer the potential for higher rental income compared to single-family homes due to the increased number of rental units. However, managing multi-family properties requires more expertise and can be more time-consuming.

c) Commercial Buildings: Commercial buildings, such as office spaces, retail stores, or industrial warehouses, can provide stable rental income and long-term investment opportunities. However, investing in commercial properties may require a larger upfront investment and more specialized knowledge.

d) Land: Investing in land can be a long-term strategy for capital appreciation. Land values can increase over time as the surrounding area develops or as the demand for land grows. However, land investments may not generate immediate income and require careful planning and zoning considerations.

Alternative Real Estate Investments

Alternative real estate investments offer indirect exposure to the real estate market without requiring direct ownership of physical properties. These investments provide diversification and access to real estate opportunities that may not be readily available through traditional methods.

a) Real Estate Investment Trusts (REITs): REITs are companies that own and operate income-producing real estate, such as apartments, office buildings, or shopping malls. Investors can purchase shares of REITs and receive a portion of the REIT's rental income. REITs offer diversification, liquidity, and the potential for dividend income.

b) Real Estate Crowdfunding: Real estate crowdfunding platforms allow individuals to invest in real estate projects with relatively small amounts of capital. These platforms connect investors with developers seeking funding for various real estate ventures, such as renovations, construction, or property acquisitions.

c) Real Estate Investment Groups (REIGs): REIGs are private investment groups that pool funds from multiple investors to acquire and manage real estate properties. Investors in REIGs share in the profits or losses of the group's real estate investments.

d) Real Estate Debt: Investing in real estate debt involves providing financing for real estate projects or purchasing mortgage-backed securities. These investments offer the potential for fixed income and can be less volatile than direct real estate ownership.

Considerations for Real Estate Investing

When considering real estate investments, it is crucial to assess your risk tolerance, investment goals, and financial capabilities. Carefully evaluate the potential returns and risks associated with each investment option. Seek professional guidance from financial advisors or real estate experts to make informed investment decisions.

Real estate investing can be a rewarding and profitable endeavor, offering a diverse range of opportunities to generate income, build wealth, and achieve financial goals. By understanding the different types of real estate investments, carefully evaluating your risk tolerance and investment objectives, and seeking professional guidance, you can make informed decisions that align with your financial aspirations.

Chapter 10: Building a Successful Career in Real Estate

10.1. Different career paths in real estate

The real estate industry offers a diverse range of career paths, catering to individuals with varying interests, skills, and experience levels. Whether you are drawn to the dynamic world of sales, the intricate aspects of property management, or the analytical world of real estate finance, there is a career path in real estate that aligns with your aspirations. Here are the different career paths available in real estate:

1. Real Estate Agent: Real estate agents, also known as real estate brokers, are the primary facilitators of real estate transactions, representing buyers or sellers in the purchase or sale of properties. They guide clients through the entire process, from property search and negotiations to closing and beyond. Real estate agents typically work on commission-based compensation, earning a percentage of the sales price for each transaction.

2. Real Estate Broker: Real estate brokers are licensed professionals who can independently own and operate a real estate brokerage firm. They manage and oversee a team of real estate agents, providing them with training, support, and guidance. Brokers typically earn commissions from the transactions their agents close, as well as fees from sponsoring new agents.

3. Real Estate Appraiser: Real estate appraisers evaluate the value of properties for various purposes, such as mortgage lending, tax assessments, or estate planning. They analyze property characteristics, comparable sales data, and market trends to determine a fair market value. Real estate appraisers typically have a strong understanding of real estate valuation principles, market trends, and legal regulations.

4. Property Manager: Property managers oversee the day-to-day operations of residential or commercial properties. They handle tenant relations, rent collection, maintenance, repairs, and compliance with legal regulations. Property managers typically have experience in real estate management, accounting, and customer service.

5. Real Estate Investor: Real estate investors purchase properties to generate income or capital appreciation. They may invest in residential properties for rental income, commercial properties for lease income, or undeveloped land for future development. Real estate investors typically have a strong understanding of market trends, property valuation, and investment strategies.

6. Mortgage Loan Officer: Mortgage loan officers originate and process mortgage loans for individuals seeking to purchase or refinance homes. They assess borrowers' creditworthiness, guide them through the loan application process, and work with lenders to secure financing. Mortgage loan officers typically have a strong understanding of mortgage lending guidelines, underwriting standards, and financial regulations.

7. Real Estate Attorney: Real estate attorneys provide legal counsel and guidance in various real estate transactions, such as property purchases, sales, leases, and financing. They draft and review legal documents, negotiate contracts, and ensure compliance with legal regulations. Real estate attorneys typically have a strong understanding of real estate law, contract law, and property rights.

8. Real Estate Market Analyst: Real estate market analysts conduct research and analyze trends in the real estate market. They gather data on property prices, sales volume, market conditions, and economic indicators to provide insights into market trends and forecast future market performance. Real estate market analysts typically have a strong understanding of data analysis, market research, and economic principles.

9. Real Estate Developer: Real estate developers plan, develop, and manage the construction of real estate projects, such as residential communities, commercial buildings, or mixed-use developments. They oversee the entire development process, from land acquisition to financing, construction, and marketing. Real estate developers typically have a strong understanding of construction management, project finance, and market analysis.

10. Real Estate Entrepreneur: Real estate entrepreneurs identify and seize opportunities in the real estate market. They may develop innovative real estate concepts, manage real estate investment funds, or launch real estate technology startups. Real estate entrepreneurs typically have a strong combination of business acumen, creativity, and risk-taking ability.

The real estate industry offers a diverse range of career paths, catering to individuals with varying interests, skills, and experience levels. Whether you are drawn to the dynamic world of sales, the intricate aspects of property management, or the analytical world of real estate finance, there is a career path in real estate that aligns with your aspirations. With dedication, hard work, and a passion for real estate, you can build a successful and rewarding career in this dynamic and ever-evolving field.

10.2. How to advance your career

Building a successful career in real estate requires dedication, knowledge, and continuous improvement. The industry offers diverse career paths, from agents and brokers to appraisers and developers. Whether you are just starting out or looking to reach new heights, here are some strategies to help you advance your career in real estate:

1. Set Clear Goals and Develop a Strategic Plan:

- Define your long-term career goals. Do you want to become a top-producing agent, a successful broker, or specialize in a specific area of real estate?
- Develop a strategic plan outlining the steps necessary to achieve your goals. This could involve setting specific targets for transactions, acquiring new skills, or networking with key industry players.
- Regularly review and update your plan to ensure it aligns with your current goals and the evolving real estate market.

2. Continuously Develop Your Knowledge and Skills:

- Take advantage of educational resources available, such as online courses, industry conferences, and workshops.
- Stay up-to-date on market trends, legal changes, and new technologies impacting the real estate industry.
- Consider pursuing professional designations like Certified Residential Specialist (CRS) or Accredited Buyer's Representative (ABR) to demonstrate your expertise and commitment to the profession.

3. Build a Strong Network:

- Connect with other professionals in the industry, including agents, brokers, lenders, appraisers, and investors.
- Attend industry events and participate in professional organizations to expand your network and build valuable relationships.
- Utilize social media platforms to connect with potential clients, industry influencers, and thought leaders.

4. Develop Your Marketing Expertise:

- Learn about different marketing strategies effective in attracting clients and generating leads.
- Utilize digital marketing tools and online platforms to reach a wider audience and showcase your services.
- Develop a strong personal brand that effectively communicates your expertise, values, and unique selling points.

5. Focus on Client Service and Building Relationships:

- Prioritize providing exceptional client service to build trust and loyalty.
- Develop strong communication and interpersonal skills to effectively interact with clients and address their needs.
- Go the extra mile to exceed client expectations and build lasting relationships.

6. Embrace Technology:

- Utilize real estate technology tools and software to improve your efficiency, manage your listings, and communicate with clients.

- Stay informed about emerging technologies and their potential applications in the real estate industry.
- Leverage technology to streamline your workflow and enhance your overall productivity.

7. Seek Mentorship and Guidance:

- Find a mentor or advisor who can provide guidance, support, and valuable insights based on their experience.
- Participate in mentorship programs or coaching sessions to accelerate your learning and professional development.
- Surround yourself with positive and supportive individuals who can encourage you and hold you accountable for your goals.

8. Be Adaptable and Resilient:

- The real estate industry is constantly evolving, and professionals need to be adaptable to navigate changes and embrace new opportunities.
- Develop resilience to overcome challenges, learn from setbacks, and bounce back stronger.
- Maintain a positive attitude and focus on continuous improvement to achieve your goals and build a successful career in real estate.

Additional Tips:

- Develop strong negotiation skills to secure favorable deals for your clients and maximize your success.
- Be involved in your community and participate in local events to build your reputation and network within the community.

- Give back to the profession by volunteering your time and expertise to mentorship programs or professional organizations.
- Prioritize your mental and physical well-being to maintain a healthy balance and sustain your energy throughout your career journey.

By implementing these strategies and continuously striving for improvement, you can position yourself for success in the competitive and rewarding world of real estate. Remember, your career journey is unique, and personal growth and development are essential to achieving your full potential.

10.3. Achieving your long-term goals in real estate

Building a successful career in real estate can be incredibly rewarding, both financially and personally. However, achieving long-term goals in this competitive field requires dedication, strategic planning, and continuous learning.

Defining Your Long-Term Goals

The first step to achieving your long-term goals is to clearly define them. What do you want to achieve in your real estate career? Do you want to build a thriving sales team? Become a top-producing agent? Develop expertise in a specific niche?

By having clearly defined goals, you can create a roadmap for success and measure your progress along the way.

Developing Your Skills and Expertise

Real estate is a fast-paced and evolving industry. To stay ahead of the curve, you must continuously develop your skills and expertise. This includes:

- Formal Education: Consider taking courses or completing certifications to enhance your knowledge of real estate law, finance, negotiation, and marketing.
- Informal Learning: Attend industry conferences, workshops, and networking events to stay updated on current trends and connect with other professionals.
- Mentorship: Seek guidance from a successful real estate professional who can provide valuable insights and support.
- Self-Education: Dedicate time to independent learning by reading industry publications, listening to podcasts, and exploring online resources.

Building Your Network

Building a strong network is essential for success in real estate. Networking allows you to:

- Connect with potential clients and referral sources.
- Learn from other professionals and stay informed about market trends.
- Collaborate on deals and expand your business opportunities.

Actively participate in industry events, join professional organizations, and connect with other real estate professionals online and in person.

Developing a Personal Brand

In today's competitive market, establishing a strong personal brand is crucial to attracting clients and achieving success.

- Define your unique value proposition. What makes you stand out from other real estate professionals?

- Develop a consistent brand identity across all platforms. This includes your website, social media presence, marketing materials, and communication style.
- Showcase your expertise and experience. Share your knowledge and insights through blog posts, articles, social media updates, and public speaking engagements.
- Build trust and credibility. Be honest, transparent, and responsive to your clients' needs.

Embrace Technology

Technology plays a vital role in modern real estate practices. Utilize real estate technology tools to:

- Streamline your workflow and increase efficiency.
- Market your listings more effectively.
- Communicate with clients more efficiently.
- Analyze market trends and gain valuable insights.

Stay informed about the latest technological advances and adopt tools that can enhance your productivity and service offerings.

Managing Your Time and Finances Effectively

Time and financial management are crucial for successful real estate professionals.

- Create a schedule and prioritize your tasks.
- Delegate tasks and outsource work when necessary.
- Track your income and expenses to maintain financial stability.
- Invest in your professional development and marketing efforts.

Staying Motivated and Resilient

Building a successful career in real estate requires hard work, perseverance, and resilience. There will be challenges along the way, but staying motivated and focused on your goals will help you overcome them.

- Set realistic goals and celebrate your achievements.
- Find a mentor or accountability partner for support.
- Maintain a positive attitude and focus on the long term.
- Take breaks and avoid burnout.

Continuously Seeking Improvement

Never stop learning and growing in your real estate career. Strive to constantly improve your skills, knowledge, and service offerings to remain competitive in the ever-changing market.

Building a Legacy

As you achieve your long-term goals, consider how you can give back to the community and leave a positive legacy in the real estate industry. This could involve mentoring future generations of real estate professionals, contributing to industry organizations, or engaging in philanthropic activities.

By following these strategies and remaining committed to your goals, you can achieve a fulfilling and successful career in the dynamic world of real estate. Remember, success takes time, effort, and continuous learning. Enjoy the journey, embrace the challenges, and celebrate your achievements along the way.

Conclusion: Women and the Future of Real Estate

The impact of women on the real estate industry

The real estate industry has traditionally been male-dominated, but women have played an increasingly important role in recent years. Their presence has impacted the industry in various ways, leading to positive changes and paving the way for future advancements.

Historically, real estate has been a challenging field for women to navigate. They faced discrimination, limited opportunities for advancement, and entrenched gender stereotypes. Despite these obstacles, many women persevered, demonstrating their competence and dedication to the industry.

In recent decades, the participation of women in the real estate industry has steadily increased. As of October 2023, women make up 66% of realtors in the United States, according to the National Association of Realtors. This surge is driven by several factors, including:

- Shifting societal norms: Increased awareness of gender equality has led to more opportunities for women in various fields, including real estate.
- Access to education and training: More women are pursuing education and training in real estate, equipping them with the knowledge and skills needed to succeed in the industry.
- Technological advancements: Technology has facilitated communication and collaboration, making it easier for women to manage their careers and businesses.
- Rise of women-focused organizations: Organizations like the National Association of Real Estate Brokers

(NAREB) and Women in Real Estate (WIRE) provide support, mentorship, and networking opportunities for women in the industry.

The increasing participation of women has had several positive impacts on the real estate industry:

- Diversity and inclusion: A more diverse workforce brings a wider range of perspectives and experiences to the table, leading to better decision-making and innovation.
- Client focus: Women are known for their strong communication skills, empathy, and ability to build relationships. This client-centric approach fosters trust and loyalty among buyers and sellers.
- Ethical standards: Women are generally more likely to adhere to ethical standards in business practices, promoting transparency and fair treatment of clients.
- Innovation and technology: Women are driving innovation in the real estate industry, leveraging technology to streamline processes, improve market analysis, and enhance the overall customer experience.

Women have played a significant role in shaping the real estate industry for decades. Their contributions span various aspects of the industry, including:

1. As Agents and Brokers: Women represent a growing force in the real estate agent and broker community. Their presence has brought a different perspective to the industry, often emphasizing relationships, communication, and empathy. Women agents and brokers are known for their strong negotiation skills, attention to detail, and commitment to client satisfaction.

2. As Investors and Developers: Women are increasingly becoming active real estate investors and developers, driving economic growth and shaping the landscape of communities. They are bringing fresh ideas and innovative approaches to the development process, focusing on sustainability, community-building, and creating spaces that cater to diverse needs.

3. As Leaders and Mentors: Women are taking on leadership roles within the industry, serving as executives, CEOs, and board members of real estate companies. Their leadership inspires and empowers other women, creating a more diverse and inclusive industry. Additionally, many women leaders mentor and support other women entering the field, fostering a collaborative and supportive environment.

4. As Consumers and Homeowners: Women are the primary decision-makers in many real estate transactions, influencing trends and shaping the demand for different types of properties and amenities. They are also driving the growth of niche markets such as co-living and co-working spaces, catering to their evolving needs and preferences.

5. As Disruptors and Innovators: Women are emerging as leaders in technology-driven innovation within the real estate industry. They are developing new tools and platforms, utilizing data analytics, and embracing digital solutions to improve the efficiency and transparency of real estate transactions.

6. As Advocates for Change: Women are actively advocating for greater diversity, equity, and inclusion in the real estate industry. They are challenging discriminatory practices, pushing for equal pay and opportunities, and creating initiatives to support and empower women in the field.

While progress has been made, women still face some challenges in the real estate industry, including:

- Gender pays gap: Women in real estate often earn less than their male counterparts, even with comparable qualifications and experience.
- Work-life balance: The demanding nature of the industry can make it difficult for women, particularly mothers, to achieve a healthy work-life balance.
- Lack of representation in leadership roles: Women are still under-represented in leadership positions within the industry.

Despite these challenges, the future for women in real estate is bright. As more women enter the field and acquire leadership positions, we can expect to see continued progress in areas such as:

- Mentorship and support: More experienced women are stepping up to mentor and support younger professionals, paving the way for future generations.
- Empowerment and advocacy: Women are advocating for themselves and their colleagues, demanding equal pay, opportunities, and representation within the industry.
- Focus on diversity and inclusion: Companies are recognizing the importance of diversity and inclusion and are implementing initiatives to attract and retain women talent.

In conclusion, women have made significant strides in the real estate industry, overcoming challenges and contributing to its growth and success. Their impact is undeniable, and their contributions are shaping the future of this dynamic field. By addressing remaining challenges and creating a more inclusive environment, women will continue to play a pivotal role in driving positive change and innovation in the real estate industry for years to come.

The future of women in real estate

The real estate industry has historically been dominated by men, but the landscape is shifting rapidly. Women are making significant strides and contributing to the growth and diversification of the field. This trend is expected to continue, paving the way for an even brighter future for women in real estate.

Here's why the future looks promising for women in real estate:

1. **Increasing Representation:** The number of women entering and succeeding in real estate is steadily rising. Statistics show that in the US, women now represent over 60% of real estate agents, and this upward trend is evident globally. This increasing representation brings fresh perspectives, diverse skillsets, and a stronger focus on collaboration and community building.

2. **Technology as a Leveling Force:** Technology is playing a crucial role in leveling the playing field for women in real estate. Online platforms, virtual tours, and digital marketing tools provide access to information, resources, and networking opportunities that were previously limited. This democratizes access to the industry and empowers women to compete effectively.

3. **Growing Recognition and Support:** Organizations and initiatives are emerging to support women in real estate.

Mentorship programs, networking events, and educational resources are helping women overcome challenges, build confidence, and advance their careers. Additionally, increasing awareness of unconscious bias and its impact on the industry is leading to more inclusive practices and fair opportunities for all.

4. Shifting Consumer Preferences: Consumer preferences are evolving, with buyers and sellers increasingly seeking out professionals who share their values and perspectives. Women real estate professionals often excel in areas like communication, relationship building, and understanding client needs, which aligns well with these changing preferences.

5. Opportunities for Innovation and Entrepreneurship: The real estate industry is undergoing a period of significant change, offering exciting opportunities for women to become entrepreneurs and innovators. Women are leading the way in developing new technologies, prop-tech solutions, and creative marketing strategies, shaping the future of the industry.

Challenges Remain, but Progress is Undeniable

Despite the positive outlook, challenges remain. Gender bias, unequal access to capital, and childcare responsibilities can still hinder women's progress. However, the increasing awareness of these challenges and the growing commitment to creating a more equitable industry are leading to positive changes.

Looking Ahead:

The future of women in real estate is bright. By continuing to break barriers, fostering collaboration, and embracing innovation, women will play an even greater role in shaping the industry and creating a more inclusive and successful future for all.

Here are some additional thoughts on the future of women in real estate:

- Specialization: Women may find success in specializing in specific areas of real estate, such as luxury properties, green building, or niche markets that align with their interests and expertise.
- Collaboration: Collaboration between women in the industry will be key to overcoming challenges and achieving mutual success. Building strong networks and supporting one another will be crucial for women to thrive.
- Focus on Sustainability: As sustainability becomes increasingly important in the real estate industry, women can take a leading role in developing and implementing sustainable solutions, contributing to a more environmentally conscious future.
- Mentorship and Leadership: Women leaders in real estate should mentor and empower the next generation of female professionals, ensuring a strong pipeline of talent and promoting gender equality in the industry.

Overall, the future of women in real estate is full of possibilities. By harnessing their unique strengths, embracing technology, and working together, women can continue to shatter glass ceilings and achieve remarkable success in this dynamic and ever-evolving industry.